Cottage Architecture of Victorian America

Cottage Architecture of Victorian America

E. C. Hussey

DOVER PUBLICATIONS, INC.
New York

Published in Canada by General Publishing Company, Ltd., 30 Lesmill Road, Don Mills, Toronto, Ontario.

Published in the United Kingdom by Constable and Company, Ltd., 3 The Lanchesters, 162–164 Fulham Palace Road, London W6 9ER.

Bibliographical Note

This Dover edition, first published in 1994, is an unabridged republication of *Hussey's National Cottage Architecture; or, Homes for Every One. Chiefly Low-Priced Buildings for Towns, Suburbs, and Country.*, published in 1874 by The American News Company, New York. The plates were unbacked in the original edition.

Library of Congress Cataloging-in-Publication Data

Hussey, E. C. (Elisha Charles)
    [Hussey's national cottage architecture]
    Cottage architecture of Victorian America / E. C. Hussey.
       p.   cm.
    "An unabridged republication of Hussey's national cottage architecture
. . . published in 1874 by The American News Company, New York"—T.p.
verso.
  ISBN 0-486-28065-9 (pbk.)
    1. Architecture, Victorian—United States—Designs and plans. 2. Architecture, Domestic—United States—Designs and plans. 3. Architecture, Modern—19th century—United States—Designs and plans. I. Title.
NA7207.H87 1994
728′.37′0222—dc20
                                             93–46723
                                               CIP

Manufactured in the United States of America
Dover Publications, Inc., 31 East 2nd Street, Mineola, N.Y. 11501

Cottage Architecture of Victorian America

"HOMES FOR EVERY ONE."

THERE are few words in the English language that convey more sweetness to the heart of man than "Home." Could we choose from the thousand duties that call us daily to mount the creaking tread-wheel of busy life, it would be to wreath immortelles over the port-ways of the myriads of pretty homes that are found on the hill-tops, sloping lands, and in the valleys, clear across our great, broad America, from Atlantic to Pacific.

In this work it has been our aim to introduce to aspirants who live, hope, and toil with that coveted day in view—which, like the *ignis fatuus*, ever sweeps on beyond their grasp—when they may sit in a "sunny nook" of their own homes, some by-way through which, perchance, they may shorten the route, or, at least, remove a few thorns from the path of their, alas! too often life-long toil. We do not, however, wish to inspire the idea that we consider this work very near perfection, or, indeed, greatly in advance of some of the many beautiful designs that have adorned the pages of numerous books and periodicals for the past few years. We do hope, however, that there may be found in this volume such originality as shall prove of substantial interest and value to all who *search* its pages. Among the thousands of men and women that we have met during our twenty years' experience who were bending their talents to the commendable end of *owning a home*, we think we may safely say we have never found *two* who were perfectly satisfied with the same plan, although many have selected houses which were, in their main features, the same. And we do not know but we are trusting in a "vain delusion" when we hope to say here is *just the plan* for you.

We have endeavored to make every page speak for itself, aiming only to keep up a general system, by arranging in close connection such plans, etc., as are quite similar in character. The following article, which we have introduced on "Sunlight, Heat, and Ventilation," will be found thoroughly practical and deserving careful consideration.

HEALTH.

SUNLIGHT, HEAT, AND VENTILATION.

In preparing a home there is no object so desirable to attain as that of healthfulness. With a view to this matter of first importance, the location should be selected with reference to obtaining unembarrassed currents of pure air, breadth of sunlight, and facilities for complete drainage.

It is well known that the statistics of hospitals, showing the recovery of patients, present a large percentage in favor of the sunny side. There are three great natural causes—light, heat, and ventilation. In order to attain the benefits of these natural auxiliaries to health, a dwelling should be so designed as to obtain the greatest possible amount of sunlight through the openings to be used in the living rooms especially; and to accomplish this result, the rooms in which the occupants are expected to spend most of their time should be as nearly as possible located on the south or southeast side of the house. Having made use of the natural agencies for home benefits, we next look for artificial means by which to finish the work. Heating dwellings by means of open grates, or "fire-places," is almost universally considered, in point of healthfulness, the best method in use, and there is no doubt of the correctness of this impression in all cases except where an equally thorough ventilation is obtained; but the moment you obtain an equal changing of air by some other means, it ceases to be a fact. Then what is most needed is a thorough, practical mode of ventilation. In order that this matter of ventilation may be more perfectly understood, we have prepared plate No. 63; by referring to said plate, in connection with the following remarks, the reader may obtain a complete idea of the whole matter. Rarefied or heated air rapidly ascends to the ceiling or roof, as the case may allow; cold, dense, or foul air as rapidly descends to the lowest portions of the space in question. And just in proportion as the one or the other obtains, so will be found their relative positions. This fact established, it becomes a matter of convenience only as to where you place your hot-air registers; but in order to secure motion and the desired results, the foul or cold air must positively be removed. Two bodies can not occupy the same space at the same time. If you open your ventilating flue at the ceiling of your room, your heated or rarefied air pops out first, and, in fact, is all that gets out, while the foul air remains below to poison you still; and just in proportion as your vent flues approach the ceilings, just in that proportion you will fail to get rid of the nuisance. These facts at once point to the base, or floor line, as the only proper position for the ventilating registers.

By placing your ventilating registers at the *base* of the room, the whole body of air in the space is set in motion. The rarefied air arising rapidly, presses down upon the foul air below, which is being sucked out at the base by the draft of the flue, and as rapidly the entire atmosphere of the room becomes equalized, while its constant changing works the most desirable results. Where no ventilating flues are used, and the cracks in doors, walls, or windows are the only ventilators, the volume of air in the room, on admitting a heated current, is thrown into a more or less revolving motion, and the success of the heating process is compelled to depend upon the sufficiency of cracks, etc., to allow the squeezing out of the one body while the other squeezes in. Where chimneys are connected with rooms, the fire-places are very excellent ventilators, and should be kept open next the hearths or floors, allowing a space equal to 6 × 6 inches in ordinary chambers for ventilation. Where no chimneys are used, a flue should be constructed of ceiling or other boards, 4 × 9 inches, passing up through the walls and connecting with the outer air, either under the cornice or through the roof, so as to insure a draft. Where chambers are situated over each other, the same flue can be used by allowing the upper one to connect through a short flue, say five feet long. These flues must be made to communicate with the rooms by means of registers in base boards, or a group of auger holes instead of registers. Ventilating registers in flues or chimneys, placed near ceilings, should invariably be kept closed, except in cases where it is desirable to reduce too great a temperature in a rapid manner in halls, churches, schools, etc.

In the use of furnaces there should be a cold air box or conductor, connecting with the outside of the walls, in a protected position; it should pass under the main hall, and be arranged so as to operate a damper valve in it from the hall floor above. Also, so as to connect a cold air register with it between the said damper and the furnace, so that when first starting up fires, and in very cold, windy weather the cold air damper may be partially or wholly closed, and the cold air register in hall, floor of church, etc., opened, as the case may require, revolving all the air in the space to be heated through the furnace, until thoroughly heated, when the cold air registers are again closed, and the dampers opened.

All rooms on a floor may be properly warmed in this way by opening all doors to hall; or the rooms may be connected with one another and with halls by means of apertures at the ceilings and bases, and using one central hot air column and one ventilator of ample capacity for use when desired, located at the base of lowest rooms.

All practice which goes aside from the foregoing in principle, is wrong and imperfect. And just in proportion as these principles are carefully observed, will the operators economize fuel and enjoy health and comfort in their home.

As has been partially alluded to in this article, where grates or stoves are used, the heat is obtained by direct radiation, and the air is changed by the draft up the chimney through the stove or grate.

PRICES OF BUILDING MATERIALS AND LABOR,

Estimates in this work are based on the prices here given, and cost of erection in other localities will be fixed by the local prices of materials.

MASON WORK AND MATERIALS.
Stone wall, including all materials, laid dry, per foot 23 cents.
  do   do laid with mortar,   -   -   do   23 do.
Excavation, per cubic yard,   -   -   -   40 do.
Brick, per thousand, laid. Pale, $19 50 to $23 50. Hard burned, $21 to $25.
Cement, per barrel, $2 50 to $3.
Lime,   do $1 75.
Hair, per bushel,   70 cents.
Lath and plastering, including all materials, 1 coat, per square yard, 40 cents.
  do   do   do   2 coats,   do   60 do.
  do   do   do   3 coats,   do   70 do.
Laths, per thousand, $3 50 to $4 50.

   Prices for all the timber, covering, flooring and finishing lumber, per thousand feet, board measure.

FRAMING TIMBER.
Pine, $45. Sawed to order. Spruce, $25. Sawed to order.
Hemlock, $22 to $25.
Firring, 2 inches wide, 6 cents each.
Studding, 13 feet by 2 × 4 inches, 21 cents each. 3 × 4, 24 cents each.
Shingles, $8 to $10.

ROOFING.
Hemlock, 1 inch thick, $24 per thousand.
Pine, 1¼ inches thick, matched, $45 per thousand.
Spruce,   do   do $35   do
Slating, per square of 100 feet, metal extra. 1st quality of slates, $15. 2d quality, $14.
Tinning, per square of 100 feet, $11 to $13.
Leaders, 4 inches calibre, per lineal foot, 30 cents.

FLOORING.
Spruce, 5 inches wide, 1¼-inch thick, $35 per thousand, planed and matched.
Spruce, 10 inches wide, 1¼-inch thick, planed and matched, $35 per thousand,
White pine, 5 inches wide, as above, $45.
White pine, 10 inches wide, as above, $45.
Georgia pine, 3 to 5 inches wide, $60 to $80, 1¼-inch thick, planed and matched.
Hemlock, 1-inch thick, matched, $24.

FINISHING STOCK, SEASONED.
Clear white pine, $65 per thousand.
Second quality of clear pine, $40 to $50.

HARDWARE.
Nails, per cwt., $5 75.

LABOR PER DAY.
Stone Mason, $4 00.   Mason's Tender, $3 00.
Bricklayer,   5 00.   Carpenter,   3 75.
Plasterer,   5 50.   Painter,   3 50.   Laborer, $2 00.

SPECIFICATIONS

FOR DESIGNS Nos. 1 AND 1 A.

EXCAVATIONS.

CELLAR.—To be excavated under the whole house, depth shown on section.

CISTERN.—Must be excavated eight feet in diameter and ten feet deep.

VAULT.—Privy and cess-pool vault to be excavated 6×6×6 feet. Also, do any other excavating required to complete the job.

GRADING.—Raise the earth immediately around the house 12 inches above present level, and slope off in all directions nicely. Clean up and leave in neat order after work is all finished.

MASON WORK.

CELLAR AND FOUNDATION WALLS.—Must stand on good footings 4 inches below cellar bottom; lay first course around with cement 18 inches thick; carry up to the final surface-level; lay with good mortar and suitable stones for good rubble masonry, 16 inches thick; nicely point up inside. Start an 8-inch brick wall on top of stone wall, flash on the inside; carry it up to height shown on section; build of good, hard brick, lay in good mortar for the purpose, nicely point outside and strike smooth inside; properly insert cellar windows as shown.

CHIMNEYS.—Placed as shown, started on good, broad footings, built up of hard brick, lain in mortar, inside nicely pargeted, drawn over under roof on an arched bar of iron, brought out in one top, as shown; lay all above roof in cement, thoroughly flash at roof; build fire-place in parlor as shown; insert thimbles and stops in all other rooms, complete.

PIERS.—For piazza to be of hard brick, 8×8 inches, supported on good foundations, lain up in cement mortar complete, as required.

CISTERN.—Bottom to be thoroughly grouted; walls 4 inches thick, of hard brick, lain up in cement; arch to be well footed and sprung, 8 inches hard brick; build up a wall around man-hole 8 inches; carry it 4 inches above earth's surface, 20 inches in diameter; lay all brick in cement. Thoroughly cement the inside and make completely water-tight, provide it with vitrified inlet and overflow pipes; connect the inlet pipes with leaders at house walls; run the overflow pipes to discharge into a dry, stoned pit.   Provide the top of the man-hole with a substantial double-board cover—will finish 7.4 × 8 feet in clear.

PRIVY VAULT.—Must be walled up with stone lain dry, to within 18 inches of the surface of the earth, where begin to lay with cement, and complete it 6 inches above the surface.   Point up all above surface on the outside.

LATHING AND PLASTERING.

Thoroughly lath with best spruce lath all walls and ceilings on first and second floors; lay off all closets one coat and hard-finish white.   All other walls and ceilings plaster two good coats and hard-finish white; use properly prepared mortar, and put it on in best manner.   Run a 5 × 8-inch stucco cornice in hall and parlor, and set a neat center-piece in parlor.   Point up after carpenter, etc.

CARPENTER WORK.

FRAME.—To be constructed as shown in plans and sections; wall strips and floor beams placed 16 inches from centers; rafters 20 inches do.; sills 4 × 6 inches—halved at all joins.   Corner posts 4 × 4 inches; wall strips 2 × 4 inches; all openings double studded; side girts 1 × 6; plates 4 × 4, of 2 × 4 s. lap joints; floor beams 2 × 10 inches; attic beams 2 × 7.   All well bridged; rafters, 2 × 6 inches.   The entire frame to be thoroughly braced and spiked together—truss partitions.

SHEATHING.—The entire outside of the building to be sheathed with dressed hemlock boards, thoroughly nailed on.

WEATHER-BOARDING.—Over the sheathing thoroughly nail on good, clear, sound quality of narrow bevel lap siding.

ROOFING.—Cover all roofs with best sound dressed hemlock boards, well nailed on, over which put on, in the best manner, best I. C. tin; thoroughly solder and secure to roofs; run all gutters of ample capacity, and provide them with leaders of sufficient capacity to convey all water from all roofs to cistern; flash all caps complete.

CORNICES, ETC.—All cornices, columns, caps, and all other outside trim, etc., to be put up of good sound pine in a substantial manner, complete, as shown on plans, etc. All steps complete, as shown.

FLOORS.—All to be lain of best quality narrow 1-inch spruce, well dressed and matched and nailed down in best manner.   Piazza floor to be lain with narrow $1\frac{1}{4}$-inch pine, w. lead in grooves, well nailed down.   Piazza thoroughly ceiled overhead, with narrow $\frac{1}{2}$-inch ceiling complete.

WINDOWS.—All to be as shown on plans and elevations. All sash to be hung with weights, cords, and pulleys, to be $1\frac{1}{2}$ inches thick, well glazed with good strong glass, and all provided with suitable fastenings. Front door to be glazed in its upper panels.

OUTSIDE BLINDS.—To be hung to all windows on good wrought iron N. Y. hinges, and provided with good strong fastenings, all to be rolling slats, stiles $1\frac{1}{4}$ inches thick.

DOORS.—All placed as shown on plans. All closet doors to be $1\frac{1}{4}$ inches thick with good rim locks, white porcelain knobs. All outside doors $1\frac{3}{4}$ inches thick, extra mortise locks and bolts. All other doors to be $1\frac{1}{2}$ inches thick, with white porcelain knobs and good mortise locks, all four paneled and hung on good strong butts.

INSIDE FINISH, ETC.—All architraves to be neatly put up and trimmed with molded face, and back molds to break over and run on top of base; parlor richer, kitchen plain, from five to six inches.

CLOSETS.—All as shown, provided with proper shelves and abundance of wardrobe racks.

STAIRS.—Run up as shown, easy rise and tread, black walnut rail 3 inches, 8-inch newel, $1\frac{1}{2}$-inch balusters, all black walnut, thoroughly put up; cellar stairs put up of good $1\frac{1}{2}$-inch plank complete, as shown on plans.

MANTELS.—Provide and set a neat marble mantel, with summer-piece and stovepipe hole, in parlor, not to cost less than $40. Other rooms with thimbles and covers, as before described.

SINK AND PUMP.—Set up where shown, in a substantial manner, a good cast iron sink 20×30 inches, with good suction pump set on drip board. Connect pump with cistern by a $1\frac{1}{4}$-inch 3 bar pipe composite metal. Provide sink with a proper waste pipe and plug trap; run waste to discharge into privy vault.

PRIVY BOX.—Build outside privy box complete over vault, as before described; provide it with seats, door, and window complete; plaster and paint it to suit.

PAINTING.

All tin roofs thoroughly paint two good coats best mineral paint. All outside and inside wood work to be painted two best coats of white lead and linseed oil in tints to suit; use turps inside; shellac all knots, and putty up complete, as needed.

FINALLY.

Provide all materials and labor, and thoroughly complete the job in workmanlike manner, according to the plans, details, and specifications, as expressed in both, or either of them, satisfactorily to the owner.

SPECIFICATIONS

AFTER WHICH WAS CONSTRUCTED DESIGN No. 17.

EXCAVATIONS.

CELLAR.—To be excavated under the entire house, three feet deep. Trenches for foundations 18 inches broad and 6 inches deeper than cellar.

CISTERN.—Make excavation sufficient to allow the cistern to finish 8 feet in diameter in clear, and 8 feet deep under the foot of the arch.

VAULT.—Privy vault must be excavated 6×6×6 feet.

DITCHES.—Excavate for all necessary ditches for inlet and overflow pipes to cistern. Also for waste and other pipes. Also excavate for all piers.

GRADING.—After all mason work is completed, grade all earth thrown out of excavations around the house, nicely sloping off in all directions from house; raise the surface of the earth immediately around the house wall one foot above the present surface-level.

MASON WORK.

CELLAR WALLS.—Must start 4 inches below cellar bottom (in the trenches) on broad footing stones, and be lain up 16 to 18 inches thick to the final surface-line, of a good quality of stones for the purpose. Lay out and start the stone wall so as to bring the inside face flash with the inside face of the brick wall resting on it. Build up of good hard brick an 8-inch wall 3 feet high above final surface; nicely point it up outside; all walls to be well pointed up inside. Insert cellar windows as shown in plans, frames to be 2×6; sills, 3×6. Piers for veranda and steps as shown, to have good, firm foundations, to be built up proper height, 8×8 inches of best, true, hard brick. All to be lain up with best mortar for the purpose.

CHIMNEYS.—Placed as per plans, to have good, solid foundations lain in cement; lay up the shafts of good hard brick in best mortar, flues as shown. Top out all chimneys as per plans, and lay all above roofs in cement; carefully flash at roof; one flue in kitchen chimney to start from cellar, and all to be thoroughly pargeted. Thimbles with covers to be inserted in three principal rooms upon second floor. Stud out chimney breasts as shown.

MANTELS, ETC.—Dining-room to have a $35 mantel, with a summer-piece and stovepipe hole extra. Parlor to have a $50 mantel, with summer-piece and stovepipe hole extra. Mantels selected by owner. Room over parlor to have a neat marble shelf on brackets to suit, with thimble and cover. All to be thoroughly and properly set.

CISTERN.—Bottom to be thoroughly grouted; wall lain up with hard brick, 4 inches thick; arch sprung on proper footings, 8 inches thick, of hard brick. Build a man-hole in center of arch 20 inches in diameter, with an 8-inch wall carried up 4 inches above final surface, and covered with a strong circular plank cover double. Thoroughly cement top of arch and outside of man-hole wall before filling in earth. Top of arch must be 16 inches below surface. Properly insert a 4-inch inlet, vitrified pipe; lay it with cemented joints to house walls, so as to connect with leaders. Also properly insert a 4-inch vitrified overflow pipe; lay it to connect with a pit 10 feet away from cistern, said pit to be 4×4×4 feet, walled up with stone lain up dry, drawn to point and keyed, finishing 12 inches below surface. Entire inside of cistern, etc., must be thoroughly cemented and made perfectly water-tight. A four-bar "composite metal" pipe must be properly inserted in cistern and connected with pump at sink in kitchen, as shown, in complete manner.

PRIVY VAULT.—To be walled up with good broad stones for the purpose, lain dry, 18 inches thick; 20 inches of the top to be lain in cement; 8×8 inch brick wall on top, above surface of earth.

DRAINAGE.—Lay a 3-inch vitrified drain pipe from house wall to privy vault; cement the joints; properly connect with it all waste pipes from house, etc.; use a plug trap at sink.

LATHING AND PLASTERING.

All interior walls and ceilings, except cellar and attic, to be thoroughly and truly lathed with good spruce lath. All closets to be lain off one good coat and hard-finished white. All rooms and halls to be thoroughly plastered two good coats and hard-finished white. Neat 5×8 inch cornices to be properly run in hall, parlor, and dining-room. Properly set neat, approved center-pieces in hall, parlor, and dining-room. Plaster privy one good coat and hard-finish white.

CARPENTER WORK.

FRAME.—To be constructed in the semi-balloon style, as per sections, plans, and details. All studs and floor beams to be 16 inches apart; sills 4×8 inches, halved and spiked together; corner posts 4×4 inches; wall strips 2×4 inches. All openings double studded; side girts 1×6. Plates 4×4 inches, made by running 2×4 inch double and lap joints; first and second floor beams 2×10 inches; attic do. 2×8 inches; rafters 2×6 inches. The entire frame to be thoroughly spiked together with 5-inch spikes. All partitions to be thoroughly trussed. Cellar girt 6×8 inches, on 8×8-inch hard brick piers, as shown.

TIMBER.—To be best quality of hemlock, free from dry rot or wind shakes.

SHEATHING.—The entire outside of the frame must be thoroughly sheathed with good, sound, dressed, and edged hemlock boards, from bottom of sills to peak of roofs, securely nailed on with 10d. nails, over which thoroughly nail on good, clear quality of narrow lap siding, from water-table up to cornices, all around.

ROOFS.—All main roofs to be thoroughly covered with best tarred roofing felt paper, lapped double, over which nail on, with 6d. galvanized nails, best medium size Chapman slate, in patterns to suit. Cope at ridges with sheet zinc. Lay all valleys broad, with sheet zinc, and make all perfectly water-tight. Bay, veranda, hoods, and roofs slated on side; pitch as shown; decks of same thoroughly tinned, flashed at walls, etc., complete. Run deep gutter around veranda, as per detail; connect a 2-inch tin conductor to the same, and make to discharge into cistern inlet pipes. Construct across rear mid-roof eave a 4×4 inch gutter, and connect in with cistern inlet pipes by a 3-inch tin leader. South side eaves drop to ground.

CORNICES.—Eave trim, dormer hoods, balcony, finials, etc., with their brackets, all to be well put up of good sound pine, in a substantial manner.

FLOORS.—All to be lain with best sound narrow 1-inch dressed and matched spruce flooring boards, thoroughly nailed down, with nails counter-sunk. Cull best boards for parlor floor, and use the poorest for attic. Veranda floor to be lain with 1¼-inch narrow pine, leaded grooves, well nailed down; steps do.

WINDOWS.—All as per plans, etc. All sash 1½ inches thick, hung in box frames, with cords, weights, and pulleys, in a substantial manner. Sash all glazed with best French sheet glass. Front door glazed in upper panels with neat-figured enameled glass, to suit. Bay window and window from parlor to veranda to be paneled down to floor. All other windows to finish on sills and stools. All windows to be properly provided with neat, strong fastenings.

BLINDS.—All windows, including cellar windows, to be furnished with good strong outside blinds; rolling slats; blinds 1¼ inches thick, hung on strong N. Y. wrought blind hinges, and provided with proper fastenings, to suit.

DOORS.—All closet doors 1¼ inches, with rim locks. All outside doors 1¾ inches thick, extra bolts and mortise lock with night-latch; cellar door rim lock and bolt in hall. All other doors 1½ inches thick, with mortise locks. All furniture, knobs, etc., to be of a good, substantial character, to suit. Sliding doors mounted on sheves and brass railway, with double furniture. Outside door double furnished and provided with gong bell and pull, properly put up. All doors thoroughly hung on good, strong butts.

SCUTTLE DOOR to attic, over B in upper hall, to be 2½ × 3 feet, with proper casing; hinged to lift over on one side, provided with a neat step-ladder, complete. Sliding door to kitchen and dining-room; closet as shown, with knob.

TRIM.—All architraves on first floor to be 7 inches, neatly molded; base do. 9 inches do.; kitchen plain. All on second floor to be 6 inches, neatly molded; base do. 7 inches do. All to be put up in a workmanlike manner, of good, sound lumber. All outside trim, etc., as shown in plans and details, to be done in a substantial manner.

CLOSETS.—All to be completely shelved and amply provided with wardrobe hooks where desired by owner.

STAIR-CASE.—Construct with easy rise, tread, and sweep, as shown; 10-inch octagon and turned newel; 3¼-inch rail; 1½-inch balusters—all black walnut. Panel up under string along side cellar stairs. Construct cellar stairs of 1¼-inch rough plank, strong and complete.

WASH-TRAYS.—To be put up in kitchen as shown; 1¾-inch stuff; leaded joints; brass plug waste. One lid to cover both trays, to be movable. Waste pipes to connect with sink waste.

SINK AND PUMP.—Sink properly set up where shown, 18 × 24 inches, provided with waste and plug trap, complete. Waste to run and discharge into privy vault. Set up at sink on drip board a No. 2 suction pump, properly connected by 3-bar 1½-inch pipe with cistern. Leave all in complete working order.

OUTSIDE PRIVY.—To be built over vault 5 × 5 feet, 8 feet high, neat roof. Plaster inside and provide with proper seats, door, and window, complete.

PAINTING.

All outside wood and tin work to be thoroughly primed with linseed oil and white lead, and painted two good coats, in tints to suit, with best Atlantic white lead and linseed oil. Privy do. All knots shellacked before priming; all nail holes and checks, etc., well puttied up after prime. All inside wood work to be painted with best white lead and turps, two good coats. All knots shellacked, and all puttied up complete after prime. Front door neatly grained, to suit.

FINALLY.

Do all that is necessary to provide materials, labor, and cartage to fully and completely finish the above in a thorough, workmanlike manner, according to the plans and specifications, to the full intent and meaning thereof expressed or implied in either.

SPECIFICATIONS

AFTER WHICH WAS ERECTED DESIGN No. 26

———▸•◼•◂———

Location will be designated by owner. Dimensions, etc., will be found on plans, details, and within.

EXCAVATIONS.

CELLAR.—Must be excavated under the whole house, to the depth of 3 feet 6 inches. Excavate for outside cellar entrance under back entrance to kitchen. Also for all piers to verandas, steps, etc.

CISTERN.—To be excavated in position shown by owner, 10 feet in diameter and 10 feet deep. Also a pit for overflow from cistern 6 feet deep and 4 feet in diameter.

CESS-POOL AND PRIVY VAULT.—To be excavated where desired by owner, 8×8 feet and 6 feet deep. Also open all ditches for all drainage required in connection with cistern, cess-pool, and well pipes, or drainage from cellar, as required.

WELL.

To be dug where desired by owner. Must be sunk to living springs; shaft of the usual diameter, to be stoned up in a thorough manner; lay 2 feet of the top of the wall of good broad stones in cement mortar. (May use cement well pipe instead of stone, if preferred.) Cover the well with a double board platform, in a thorough manner, and provide with a first-class chain pump, properly set up and left in complete working order, satisfactory to the owner.

MASON WORK.

FOUNDATION WALLS to start 4 inches below cellar bottom in trenches, 20 inches broad, bed in cement, 12 inches high.

CELLAR WALLS to start on foundations as above, to be built of good quality of stones for rubble walls. All to be started so as to bring the inside of the walls flush on the inside. Must be well bonded together, 18 inches thick, lain up with good mortar, composed in proportions of two barrels of lime to one of cement, and properly united with clean, sharp sand; point up smoothly on the inside, and on the outside where exposed to view. Set foundations for all piers, posts, etc., with broad, flat stones, lain in cement. Build area wall and steps for outside cellar entrance, complete, of stone and brick. Build all piers for verandas, steps, etc., 8 inches square, proper height, of best hard brick, lain up in cement. Cellar walls, from bottom of cellar, will be 7 feet high, to bottom of sills.

CHIMNEYS.—Place them as shown on plans. Start them 4 inches below cellar bottom, on best foundations. Build them of good hard brick. Start one flue in each from cellar, and one from each room through which the chimneys pass. Build kitchen chimney for Warren's elevated range, which will be furnished by owner. Properly set said range where shown on plans, and provide with a smooth stone hearth. Prepare all chimneys for grates and mantels where shown on plans. Properly set said grates, and provide with rubbed stone hearths, sizes shown. All flues must be smoothly pargeted. Lay all chimneys up with good mortar, and all above roofs in best cement, and top them out as per plans. Thoroughly flash all chimneys at roofs. Provide and conduct a hot-air flue from kitchen range to register in bath-room in usual manner. Conduct smoke from range through a 6-inch vitrified pipe, built up with chimney as shown. Carry it up as high as attic floor. Substantial headers to be framed around all chimneys, and *no portion* of the frame must be allowed to take bearing on any of the chimneys.

CISTERN.—Grout the cellar bottom in the best manner. Build the walls of best hard brick 4 inches thick, circular form; thoroughly foot and spring an 8-inch arch so as to finish 20 inches below surface-level. Build up wall 8 inches thick around man-hole, which will be 20 inches in diameter. Lay up all the brick in cement, best quality; cement man-hole and arch outside before filling in the earth. Thoroughly plaster with best cement the entire cistern, etc., and make it perfectly water-tight; properly insert inlet and overflow pipes (vitrified), 4 inches in diameter. Lay 4-inch vitrified pipes in cement, with conductors from gutters, so as to convey all water from all roofs to the cistern, in a thorough manner. Stone up "overflow pit," which will be placed 15 feet from cistern, size as above, with dry-lain stones drawn to an arch at top, thoroughly keyed and covered over 18 inches below the surface of the earth. Lay 4-inch overflow pipe from cistern, and connect with pit in a thorough manner. Cistern finish 9 feet 4 inches in diameter and 8 feet under arch. Provide cistern with substantial cover, made of 1-inch boards, doubled and crossed.

CESS-POOL AND PRIVY VAULT.—To be where directed; thoroughly wall with best stone for the purpose. Lay up dry to within 20 inches of the surface of earth, where commence to lay with cement and so finish up 8 inches above the final surface-level. Lay a 6-inch vitrified pipe from house, which will be connected with soil pipes, and properly connect with vault. Cement the joints; lay with descent of an inch to 16 inches.

DRAINAGE.—Provide and lay a 3-inch tile drain through the center of the cellar from front to rear, 6 inches below grouting.

GROUTING.—Thoroughly grout and cement the entire cellar bottom. The foundation of piers for posts in cellar to finish 4 inches above grout.

LATHING AND PLASTERING.

All interior walls and ceilings on first and second floors, in attic hall, and in tower attic room, to be thoroughly lathed with best spruce lath, well nailed on all angles, thoroughly keyed; all walls plumbed and ceilings leveled, and all, except closets, to be thoroughly plastered two good coats, and finished with hard-finish white, in best manner. All ceilings ditto. All closets to be laid off one good coat and hard-finished white. Spring ellipse across hall, where shown; face it on neat corbels to suit. Also spring ellipses across all bays, footed on corbels. All corners of bays, and piers under hall ellipses, to have rule-joint bead on them. Parlor, lower hall, library, and dining-room to be run with neat 7×9 inch cornices, and all provided and set with neat, approved centers in stucco, to be selected by owner, all to suit. No cornices on second floor. Vestibule to have cornice and center to suit. All materials and workmanship to be of the best quality for all above work. Also thoroughly lath and plaster the entire cellar ceiling one good coat of properly prepared mortar. Lay it off smooth and whitewash it; run it completely tight up to side walls, and stop all air-holes under sills.

CARPENTER WORK.

FRAME.—To be executed in the semi-balloon style, as shown in section and details.

TIMBER.—To be best quality of hemlock or spruce, dry, sound, and free from wind shakes.

SIZES.—Sills 4×8 inches, halved and spiked together at angles and joints. Girts 6×6 inches. Corner posts 4×6 inches. Wall strips 2×4 inches. All openings double studded; side girts 1×6 inches, gained and spiked into wall strips flush. Plates 4×4 inches, made by running two corners 2×4, lap joints. First and second floor beams 2×10 inches. Attic beams 2×8, all thoroughly double bridged. Rafters 2×6 inches, well supported over wall. The entire frame to be thoroughly spiked together with 5-inch spikes and 12d. nails. All partitions thoroughly trussed. All floor beams, wall strips, and attic beams to be 16 inches apart. Rafters 20 inches apart. French roof portion framed as shown.

SHEATHING.—The entire outside of the frame and roof to be thoroughly sheathed with best single-faced hemlock boards, thoroughly nailed on from sills to peak on ridge of roof; over which tack on best tarred felt paper, edges well lapped, sides and roofs complete.

SIDING.—To be best narrow white pine lap bevel siding, to be well nailed on over felt. Flash all veranda, bay, and hood roofs, window caps, etc., with sheet zinc.

ROOFS.—All constructed as shown in plans. Decks all covered with best C. C. tin, well secured to roof, and thoroughly flashed and soldered and made water-tight. All bay windows and piazza roofs ditto. Batter roofs to be thoroughly slated with best non-fading purple slate, medium sizes for the purpose, put on with 8d. galvanized nails. Band through center of roof horizontal, one-third its depth to be cut octagon ends. Tower roofs carefully tinned and flashed at sides, and made perfectly water-tight. All flashings to be sheet zinc.

GUTTERS.—To be constructed on deck cornice, as shown. Piazza cornices and gutters as shown, all to have proper drain, and to be intersected with

LEADERS of sufficient capacity to carry off all water readily without overflowing; leaders to connect with pipes as above to cistern, so as to convey all water thereto. Great care must be taken with all

VALLEYS to flash them thoroughly with sheet zinc.

CORNICES and tower finish, all as shown in plans and details, to be thoroughly put up of good dry white pine, well secured.

FLOORS.—First and second floors, attic hall, and tower room, to be covered with best quality of narrow spruce flooring boards, dressed, tongued, and grooved, full inch thick, thoroughly lain and nailed down, closely and completely cut in between wall strips. Attic garret to be floored with matched and single-dressed hemlock boards complete, well nailed down. Verandas and stoop to be floored with best 5-inch pine, dressed and matched plank, 1¼ inches thick, thoroughly lain in white lead joints and blind nailed complete. Tower top floor will be raised 4 feet above rest of attic floor, and reached by steps, as shown in plans.

HOT-AIR TUBES.—To be provided and properly set up in walls where shown, constructed of tin, and spaces between studs tin-lined around pipes; all to be thoroughly done and left complete, communicating with cellar, ready for connection with furnace.

Provide and set registers with valves, etc., complete where shown, and of sizes shown and figured on plans.

GAS PIPES.—Run proper gas pipes to light the house throughout, for center lights in parlor, hall, library, dining-room, and kitchen, with light on newel post, first hall; all side lights up-stairs; arrange to connect with main from street. (See notes on plans.)

WINDOWS.—All to be of sizes and forms shown in plans, details, etc. Cellar windows all to have 1½-inch sash, glazed with good strong glass; sash to be hung at side with strong butts; sills to be 3-inch chestnut or oak. All other sash to be 1½ inches, glazed with best French sheet glass. All hung with cords, weights, and pulleys, complete, in box frames, and provided with good, approved fastenings. All windows from parlor, library, and dining-room opening on piazza to run down to the floors, lower sash to have loose heads, so as to shove up to meeting rail; front vestibule doors glazed with neat-figured and enameled glass, as shown. Transom over side hall door; small lights in the gables of attic, as shown, hinged so as to open in. All bays to be paneled to floor, neatly. All other windows, not otherwise specified, to finish on stools, sills, and aprons, complete; rear tower window one sash only, as shown, to drop behind ceiling board screen.

BLINDS.—All windows to be provided with outside blinds 1¼ inches thick; cellar windows also, rolling slats, hung with best N. Y. hinges, and provided with best fastenings, to suit; all openings in pairs. No blinds on the three small gable windows.

DOORS.—All as shown on plans; outside cellar door 1¾ inches thick, hung and provided with bolts; sash door to "milk room" 1¼ inches. All closet doors single molded, 1¼ inches thick, all provided with good rim locks and white porcelain knobs and silver-plated shanks and furniture. Sliding doors as shown, 1½ inches thick, elliptical heads, mounted on brass rails, with best sheaves, furnished with best white porcelain knobs, locks, etc., complete, double furniture. All outside and vestibule doors 1¾ inches thick, provided with good mortise locks, bolts, etc., complete, extra bolts on outside doors, inside; all trimmed and furnished same as sliding doors; all other doors 1½ inches thick, mortised locks, same furniture, etc., as above. All doors to be hung on good strong loose butts to suit, and all left in complete working order. Panel moldings in doors on first floor (except kitchen) to be raised black walnut.

CASINGS, INSIDE TRIM, ETC.—All to be thoroughly executed according to the plans, etc., lower story base 9 inches high.   Second do. 8 inches, all neatly molded.   (See sizes of doors on plans, etc., and see plans and details.)   Kitchen finish plainer. All saddles to be black walnut.

CLOSETS.—(See plans.)   To be shelved throughout as directed.   All up-stairs to be provided with a great abundance of wardrobe hooks, complete.   Kitchen closets and china do. to be provided with cupboard, as shown, doors over, and three drawers under.   (See plans.)

STAIR-CASES.—As shown; run all stairs complete; $1\frac{1}{4}$-inch tread; $\frac{7}{8}$-inch rise; 4-inch black walnut rail; 2-inch balusters; 10-inch newel, with gas column on top of it.   Stairs to attic inclosed as shown.   Closet under cellar stairs as shown.   Stairs up into tower room with rail and baluster guard, as shown.   Stairs to stoop and piazzas complete, as shown, $1\frac{1}{2}$-inch tread, 1-inch rise; inclose cellar way under main stairs, with paralleled ceiling.   Return-nosings and trim on string to steps.

MANTELS AND GRATES where shown, all to be provided by owner, and set in complete working order by builder.

WAINSCOTS of black walnut and ash to be put up in the bath-room and kitchen complete, 2-inch strips, or less, 30 inches high, neatly coped above base.   Kitchen wainscots to be $4 \times \frac{7}{8}$ inch, clean pine, beaded and coped neatly.   All to be nicely smoothed off and wax-oiled and varnished same as other work.

FINISH OUTSIDE.—All outside finish to be well and thoroughly put up, of good dry white pine, according to the plans and details, which see.   Dormers, cornices, brackets, columns, balusters on veranda, etc., all complete, finials as shown, thoroughly secured to the building.   Veranda ceiled under with narrow pine ceiling boards, and painted to suit.

"MILK ROOM" in cellar partitioned off with ceiling boards, tongued and grooved complete, and supplied with shelves.

PLUMBING, HEATING, ETC.

TANK.—Construct and securely arrange and support in garret where shown, a tank 4×8 feet and 3 feet deep.   Thoroughly line it with "medalion metal," of good weight (say gauge 25) for the purpose.   Make connection from tank to range with 3-bar composite metal pipe $\frac{5}{8}$ of an inch.   Also with force and lift pump to tank, same quality pipe.   Also insert an overflow 2-bar pipe 4 inches from top of tank, and conduct it to discharge into leader; do all the plumbing necessary in a most thorough manner.   Also to connect tank with wash-bowl, bath-room, and water-closet with 3-bar pipe; provide lid with lock to tank. Also insert a discharge pipe in bottom of tank, with good cock, to connect with leaders so as to draw off all water at will and protect it. Provide all supply pipes from tank to other works, with cut-off cocks at tanks, and protect them by casing up.

BATH-ROOM.—As shown, to be thoroughly fitted up with tub, wash-basin, and water-closet. Bath-tub to be thoroughly lined with medalion metal, lighter than tank, and plumbed with hot and cold water, in a complete manner, and connected with range by 3-bar pipe; with tank ditto. Wash-basin to have marble top and bowl and waste plug as shown, cased up with black walnut, supplied with hot and cold water complete, same as tub, with waste and trap. Water-closet plumbed with earthen-ware basin, and pan trap, with silver-plated pull and cup complete; supplied with water as above. All cocks required in bath-tub and wash-basin to be good, substantial silver-plated-ware, of suitable character. All cocks required to complete plumbing in kitchen at sink, boiler, pump, waste-traps, etc., to be burnished brass, of a good, substantial, suitable character. Connect a 5-inch cast iron soil pipe with water-closet; convey it down walls and connect with soil drain to cess-pool. Swedge lead the joints. Connect waste pipes with bath-tub, and wash-basin with traps, and discharge into water-closet. Closet bowl and tub to be neatly cased up with black walnut, double flap cover to closet. Also provide bath-tub and wash-basin with overflow, and connect with waste complete; waste from tub, 1½ lead pipe.

SINK.—Where shown in kitchen, fitted up with drip board, plumbed with hot water from range, 3-bar pipe; connect waste 1½-inch, with plug, trap, and conduct it to discharge into soil drain. Arrange pump to discharge into sink. Sink to be galvanized iron. Set sink on 6-inch string board with nosing; do not case under; do all plumbling in a thorough manner.

PUMP.—Set in kitchen where shown a first-class No. 4 2¾-inch force and lift pump. So plumb it as to connect with cistern by 3-bar pipe, composite metal; also with well to force water from either to tank in attic. Also to discharge water at will into sink; make all cut-offs to accomplish the same, so as to readily reach them at the pump. Discharge water from pump into sink through a screw nozzle, and provide a rubber tube with fittings so as to pass water to either of the wash-trays at will through said tube, it being screwed into pump nozzle.

WASH-TUBS.—Where shown in kitchen, to be thoroughly constructed in the usual manner of 1¾-inch pine plank, with covers complete, plumbed with hot and cold water, provided with waste plugs, chains, and waste pipe; waste pipe to discharge into waste drain. Also provide overflow pipe set 6 inches from top connected with waste pipe; waste pipe 1½ inches.

RANGE.—Set in kitchen, as shown, a Warren's elevated range, to be furnished by owner, with water back, etc. Do all plumbing to connect with other works as before specified. Set up on stool a forty-gallon planished copper boiler, and make all connections as above noted. Finally, do all plumbing required in plans and specifications in a thorough, complete manner, using good, strong composite metal pipe and medalion metal as before named, and leave all in complete working order.

REGISTERS.—All as before named, where shown.

BELLS AND TUBES.—Bells from front bed-rooms to servant's room, and from front door, hung in kitchen, provided with suitable pulls, and connected with steel wire. Also put up speaking-tube from upper hall to kitchen, with mouth-pieces and whistle complete. Also bell complete from library to kitchen.

STAINING.—All interior woodwork to be carefully puttied and smoothed up, and stained with wax and oil, containing such stain as desired, either light oak, satinwood, or walnut stain; some of the trim on second floor stained black walnut. After it is thoroughly dry, varnish two good coats with best hard varnish; putty must be the color of the stain.

PAINT.—All outside woodwork to be thoroughly painted two good coats of best white lead and linseed oil in tints to suit; front and vestibule doors to be neatly grained to suit owner. All tinwork treated in same way. Roofs, gutters, etc., two coats best mineral paint for purpose to suit.

OUTSIDE PRIVY to be built over vault of cess-pool; to be 6×6 feet; tin and slate roof, to suit style of house; finished with seats, paper-box, etc., complete; inside door and lock, window, etc.; lathed and plastered, sided like house, and painted inside and outside two good coats, same as house. Where figures occur on the plans, follow them instead of the scale.

FINALLY.

Do all that is necessary to provide all materials, labor, and cartage to fully complete, in a workmanlike manner, according to the plans, specifications, and details, to the full intent and meaning thereof as expressed or implied in either or all of them, satisfactory to the owner.

GENERAL REMARKS.

WITHOUT entering into the detail of "cause and effect," we have here appended a few statements and suggestions, with somewhat the air of self-evident facts, that may have been drawn out by interrogations; and we assure our readers that they may be implicitly relied upon as the best known practice, embodying (all things else being equal) the greatest economy and durability. Foundations should always be placed under the superstructure so as to bring the cellar walls flush on the inside, instead of having an off-set where the brick and stone meet at surface, as is very common. Walls frequently bow in, but never out; the above will avoid it. Use great care to thoroughly bed the stone, so as not to rest on the mortar, especially where one portion of the wall is of necessity higher than the rest, as very considerable shrinkage takes place in stone walls. Grouting over the sills between beams thoroughly is a trifling expense and of great benefit. Cisterns should always be put in when foundations are complete and ready to take the first water from the roofs, both for the convenience of the water and the certainty of having the cistern ready and in order. Framing is a very important consideration in house-building. The frames described in this work are far superior to the old-fashioned "skeleton" frame, which depends upon its posts, that are always half cut off, for its resistance to horizontal atmospheric pressure. Avoid to the fullest extent horizontal wood, and do not compel the partitions of the central portion of the building to be carried by or cut through with much more horizontal wood than the sills of the outside walls present. Where it is possible, use full-lengthed strips in setting partitions that are resting over each other, the object being to cause an even settling and to avoid ugly cracks at an angle of 45° (more or less). All partitions, not resting over others, should be trussed to support themselves, and the entire frame thoroughly braced and spiked together. We have known skeleton frames to break off and fall down in high winds, and cause great loss of life. We have never known such as we have described to do so. Roofs should always be constructed so as to throw all weight upon the outside walls and upon the partitions that have bearings on girders and posts below. Also use care to avoid all thrust or horizontal pressure by rafters. Crestings should never be omitted on French-roofed houses where it is possible (in a financial sense) to put them up; they are, with the finials, the principal available features of ornamentation in low-priced houses.

We know hundreds of such houses that would be enhanced in value one-fourth for a trifling outlay on crestings. Wood is generally cheapest for this purpose, but its lack of durability forbids its use; besides, it is liable to look clumsy. Iron crestings are now being furnished at very low rates, and are exceedingly ornamental. The best and most economical article we know of in this line is the "Yates" cresting, which has, added to its other virtues, that of being constructed so as to form a most complete *lightning rod*, with the addition of conductors to the earth. Lightning rods are *tabooed* by many—we know them to be of great value if properly put up, especially so in many suburbs; besides, they are of great sanitary benefit to nervous persons. Painting is a matter of protection chiefly, but is of most vital importance also in regard to the beauty of a house; there is rarely an exception where a bright lively color is not far preferable. Avoid giving your house the *blues* or the *greens* with paint.

GRADING, ETC.—Never plan to use terraces where it is possible to avoid them—they are difficult to keep and also difficult to make beautiful. Grade up well; that is, lift your house well from the common level, and slope off gently in all directions; two and a half to three feet is a good height for the bottom of the water table of a country or suburban house from the surface as established around the house. Avoid, as a rule, a great extent of walks.

Fences are generally considered essential around a house, but often destroy otherwise a very pretty place. They should never be more than forty-four inches high, and should by all means harmonize with the house and surroundings.

CONTRACT PRICE $1800.

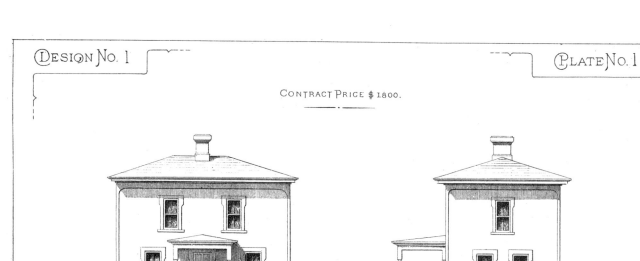

FRONT ELEVATION.   SIDE ELEVATION.

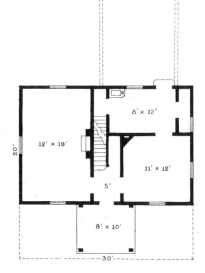

GROUND PLAN.

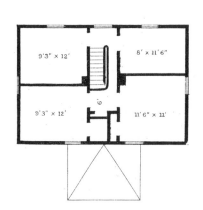

CHAMBER PLAN.

CONTRACT PRICE $1900.

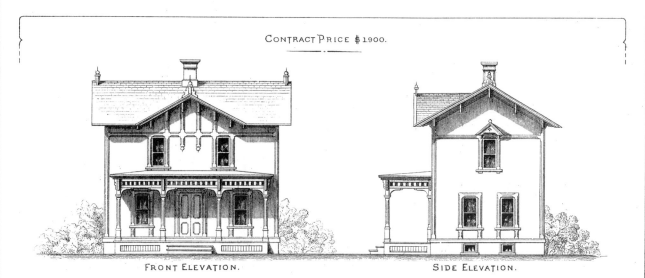

FRONT ELEVATION.   SIDE ELEVATION.

DESIGN No. 1. A.

SCALE 1/16 INCH TO 1 FOOT.   SAME PLANS AS ABOVE.

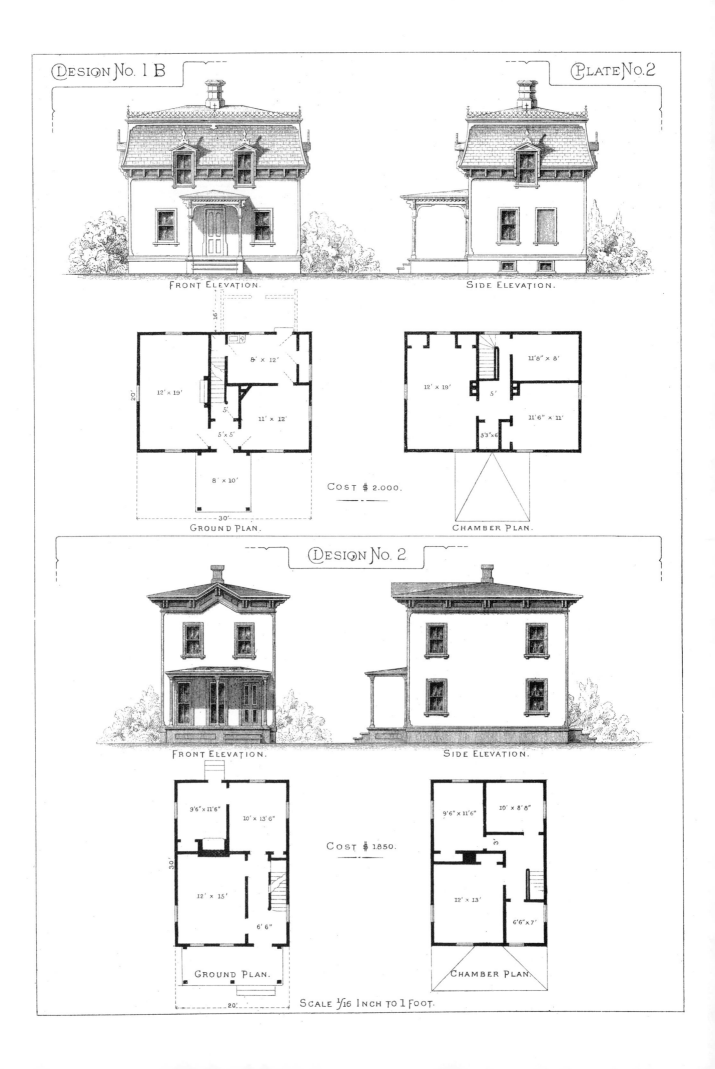

FRONT ELEVATION.

SIDE ELEVATION.

16'

8' × 12'

12' × 19'

5'

11' × 12'

5' × 5'

20'

8' × 10'

30'

GROUND PLAN.

11'8" × 8'

12' × 19'

5'

11'6" × 11'

5'3" × 6'

CHAMBER PLAN.

COST $ 2.000.

Design No. 2

FRONT ELEVATION.

SIDE ELEVATION.

9'6" × 11'6"

10' × 13'6"

30'

12' × 15'

6' 6"

20'

GROUND PLAN.

9'6" × 11'6"

10' × 8'8"

3'

12' × 13'

6'6" × 7'

CHAMBER PLAN.

COST $ 1850.

SCALE ⅟16 INCH TO 1 FOOT.

Perspective

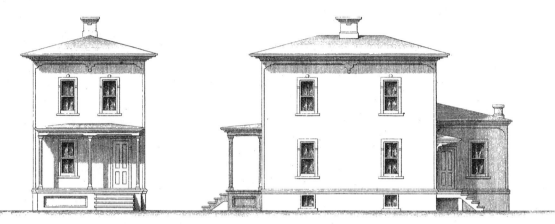

FRONT ELEVATION.   SIDE ELEVATION.

CONTRACT PRICE $ 2000.

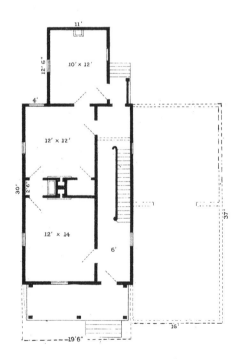

GROUND PLAN.

CHAMBER PLAN.

SCALE ⅟₁₆ INCH TO 1 FOOT

PERSPECTIVE

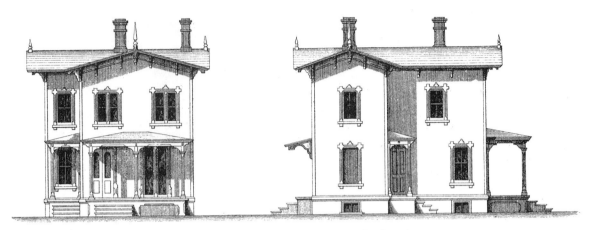

FRONT ELEVATION   SIDE ELEVATION

Was Built for $ 2900.

KITCHEN
10'6" x 12'0"

DINING ROOM
12' x 15'6"

PARLOR
12 x 13

HALL
6'6"

GROUND PLAN

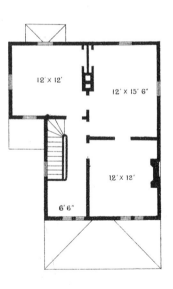

12' x 12'

12' x 15'6"

12' x 12'

6'6"

CHAMBER PLAN

Scale ⅛ inch, to 1 foot.

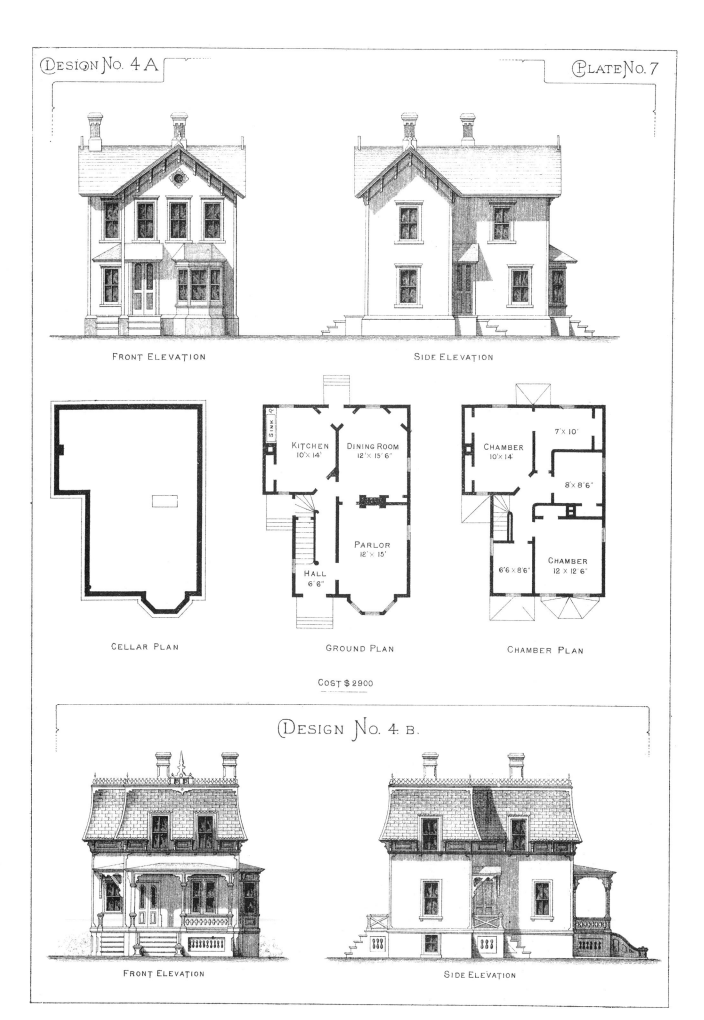

FRONT ELEVATION

SIDE ELEVATION

KITCHEN
10' X 14'

DINING ROOM
12' X 15' 6"

PARLOR
12' X 15'

HALL
6' 6"

CHAMBER
10' X 14'

7' X 10'

8' X 8' 6"

6' 6" X 8' 6"

CHAMBER
12 X 12' 6"

CELLAR PLAN

GROUND PLAN

CHAMBER PLAN

COST $ 2900

DESIGN No. 4. B.

FRONT ELEVATION

SIDE ELEVATION

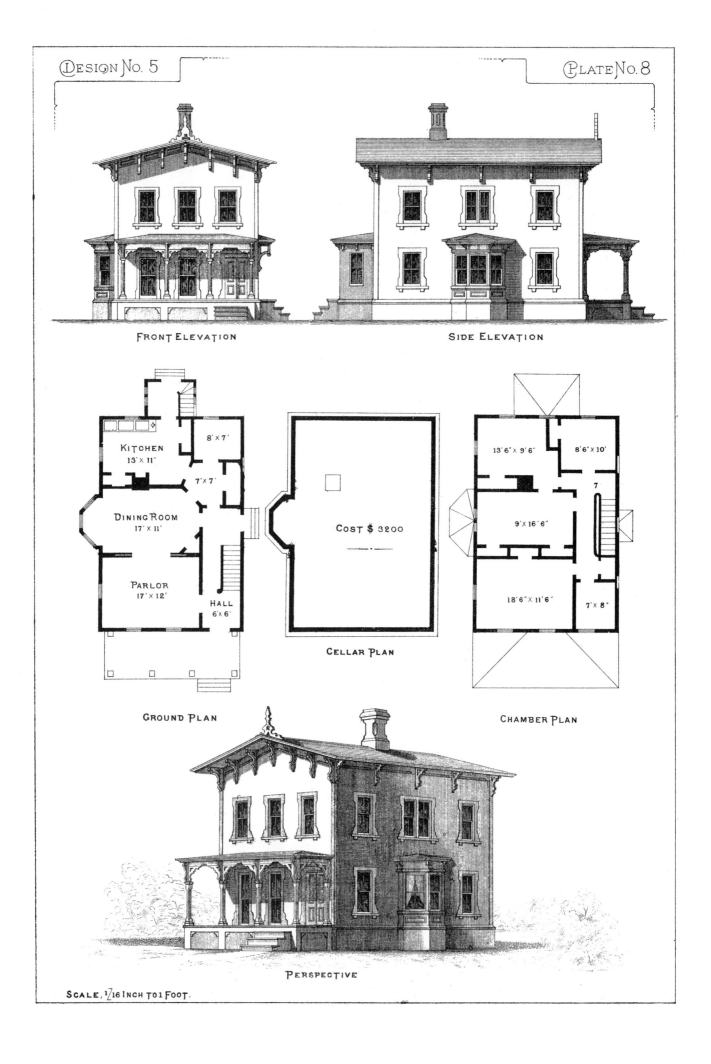

Design No. 5

Plate No. 8

Front Elevation

Side Elevation

Kitchen
13' x 11'

8' x 7'

7' x 7'

Dining Room
17' x 11'

Parlor
17' x 12'

Hall
6' x 6'

Ground Plan

Cost $ 3200

Cellar Plan

13'6" x 9'6"

8'6" x 10'

7

9' x 16'6"

18'6" x 11'6"

7' x 8"

Chamber Plan

Perspective

Scale, 1/16 Inch to 1 Foot.

SIDE ELEVATION

COST $ 4000.

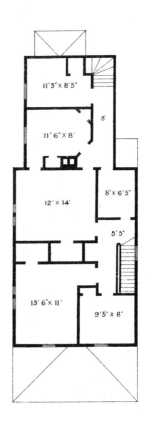

16'

KITCHEN
15' x 11' 6"

18'

DINING ROOM
17' x 12'

3' 6"

30'

PARLOR
14' x 16'

HALL
6' 6"

8'

22'

GROUND PLAN

11' 5" x 8' 5"

3'

11' 6" x 8'

12' x 14'

8' x 6' 5"

5' 5"

13' 6" x 11'

9' 5" x 8'

CHAMBER PLAN

Scale. ⅟₁₆ inch to 1 Foot.

PERSPECTIVE

FRONT ELEVATION

SIDE ELEVATION

CREST
AND
DECK CORNICE.

18'

VERANDA BRACKET,
CORNICE & POST.

CENTRE CREST FINIAL

MAIN CORNICE
AND
BRACKET.

HOODS
OVER
WINDOWS IN ROOFS.

DETAILS

1/16 Inch to 1 Inch.

PERSPECTIVE

SIDE ELEVATION.

FRONT ELEVATION.   SIDE ELEVATION

COST $4200

GROUND PLAN.   CHAMBER PLAN.

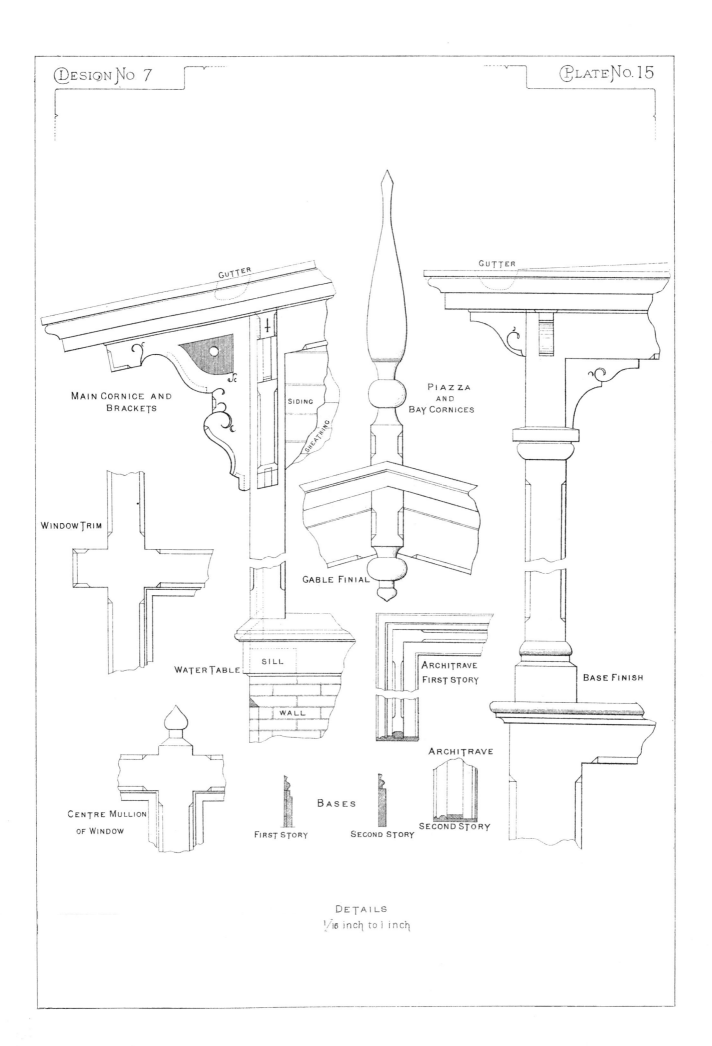

GUTTER

GUTTER

MAIN CORNICE AND
BRACKETS

SIDING

SHEATHING

PIAZZA
AND
BAY CORNICES

WINDOW TRIM

GABLE FINIAL

WATER TABLE

SILL

WALL

ARCHITRAVE
FIRST STORY

BASE FINISH

ARCHITRAVE

CENTRE MULLION
OF WINDOW

BASES

SECOND STORY

FIRST STORY

SECOND STORY

DETAILS
1/16 inch to 1 inch

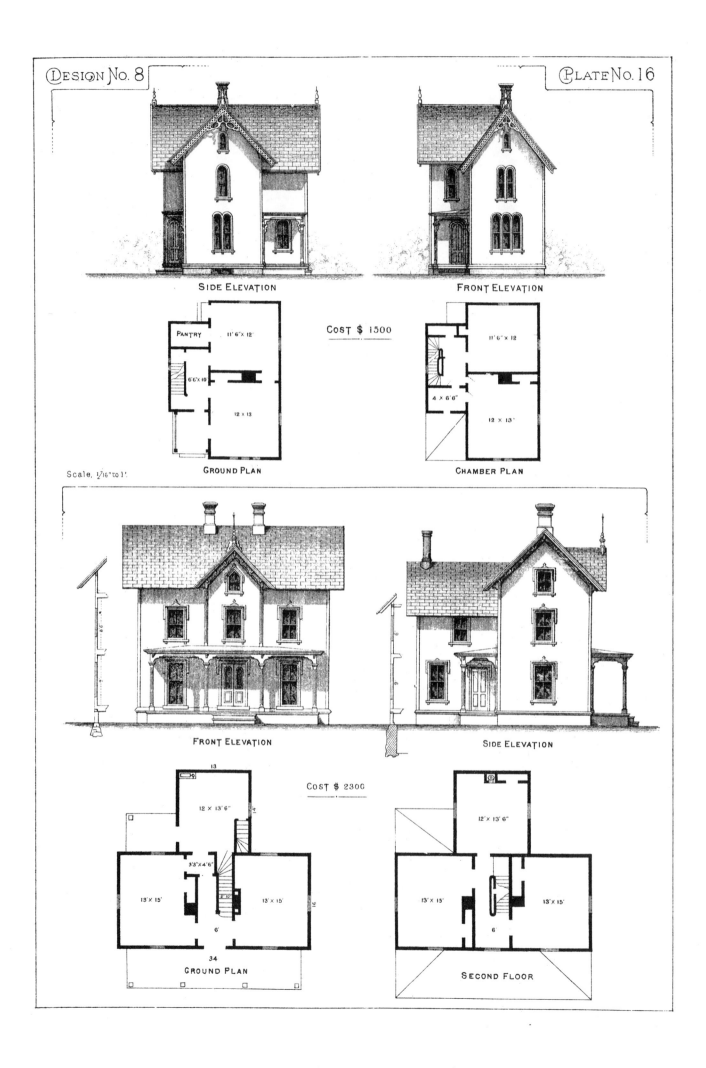

DESIGN No. 8

PLATE No. 16

SIDE ELEVATION

FRONT ELEVATION

COST $ 1500

PANTRY

11' 6" x 12'

11' 6" x 12

6' 6" x 10'

4 x 6' 6"

12 x 13

12 x 13'

GROUND PLAN

CHAMBER PLAN

Scale, 1/16" to 1'.

FRONT ELEVATION

SIDE ELEVATION

COST $ 2300

13

12 x 13' 6"

12' x 13' 6"

3' 3" x 4' 6"

13' X 15'

13' X 15'

13' X 15'

13' X 15'

6'

6'

34

GROUND PLAN

SECOND FLOOR

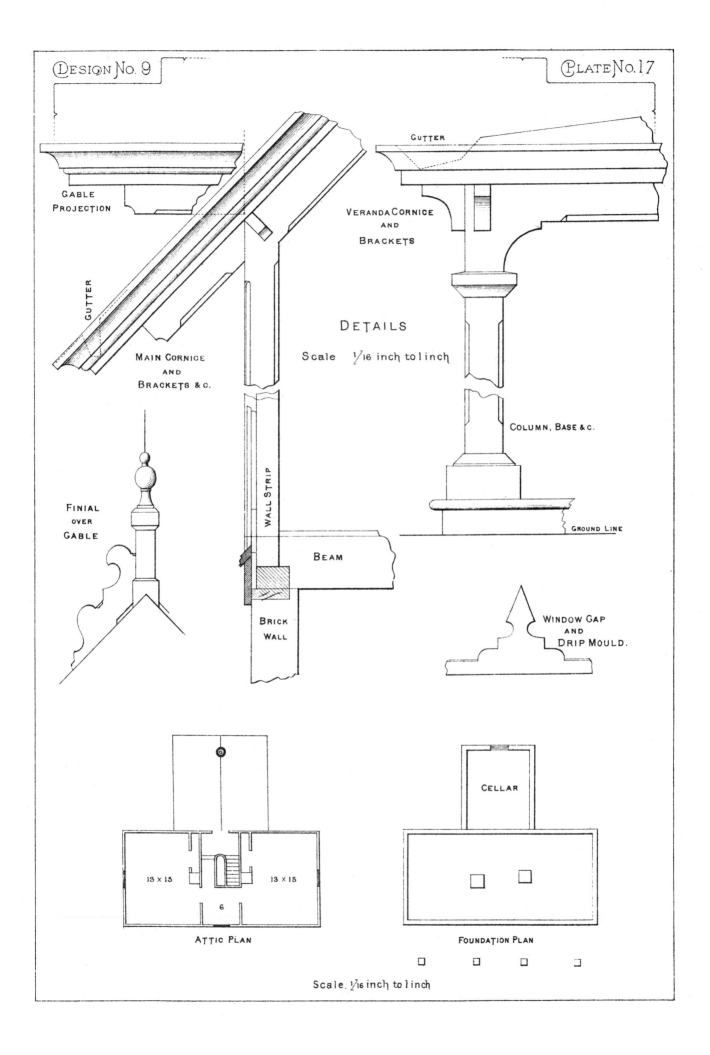

GABLE
PROJECTION

GUTTER

MAIN CORNICE
AND
BRACKETS &C.

VERANDA CORNICE
AND
BRACKETS

GUTTER

DETAILS

Scale ¹/₁₆ inch to 1 inch

COLUMN, BASE &C.

FINIAL
OVER
GABLE

WALL STRIP

BEAM

BRICK
WALL

GROUND LINE

WINDOW GAP
AND
DRIP MOULD.

13 x 15   13 x 15

6

ATTIC PLAN

CELLAR

FOUNDATION PLAN

Scale, ¹/₁₆ inch to 1 inch

PERSPECTIVE

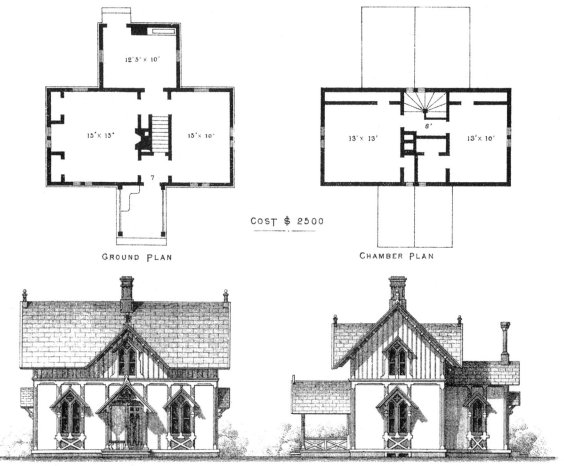

12' 5" x 10'

15' x 13'   15' x 10'

7

GROUND PLAN

13' x 13'   13' x 10'

8'

CHAMBER PLAN

COST $ 2500

FRONT ELEVATION   SIDE ELEVATION

Scale, 1/16 inch to 1 Foot.

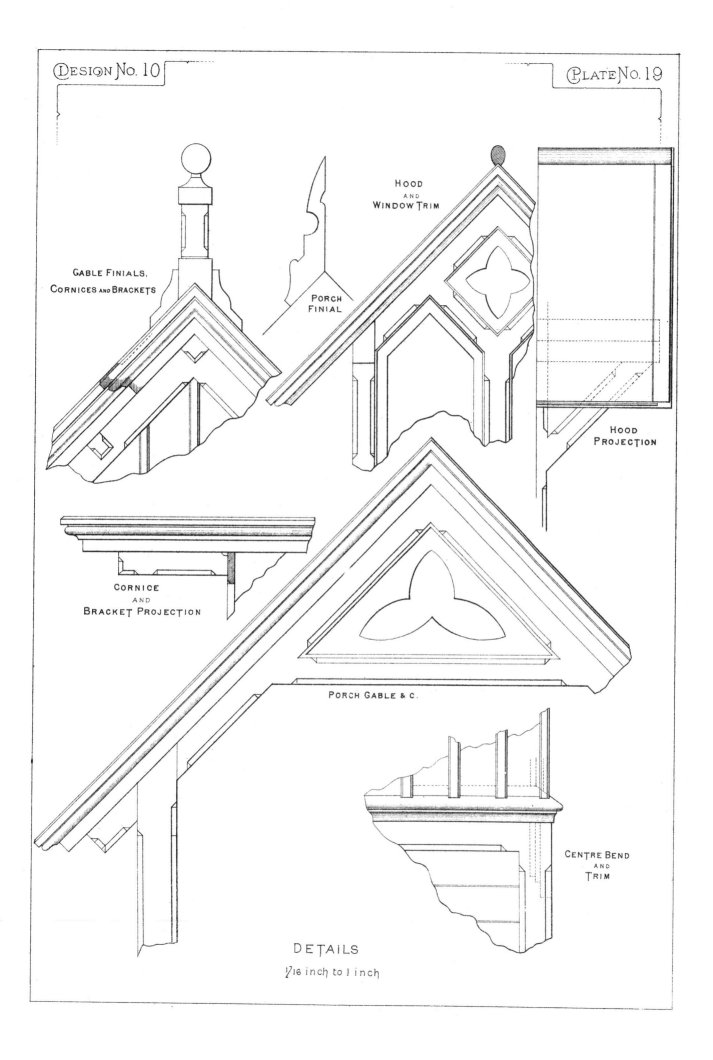

Gable Finials,
Cornices and Brackets

Porch
Finial

Hood
and
Window Trim

Hood
Projection

Cornice
and
Bracket Projection

Porch Gable & c.

Centre Bend
and
Trim

Details

1/16 inch to 1 inch

PERSPECTIVE

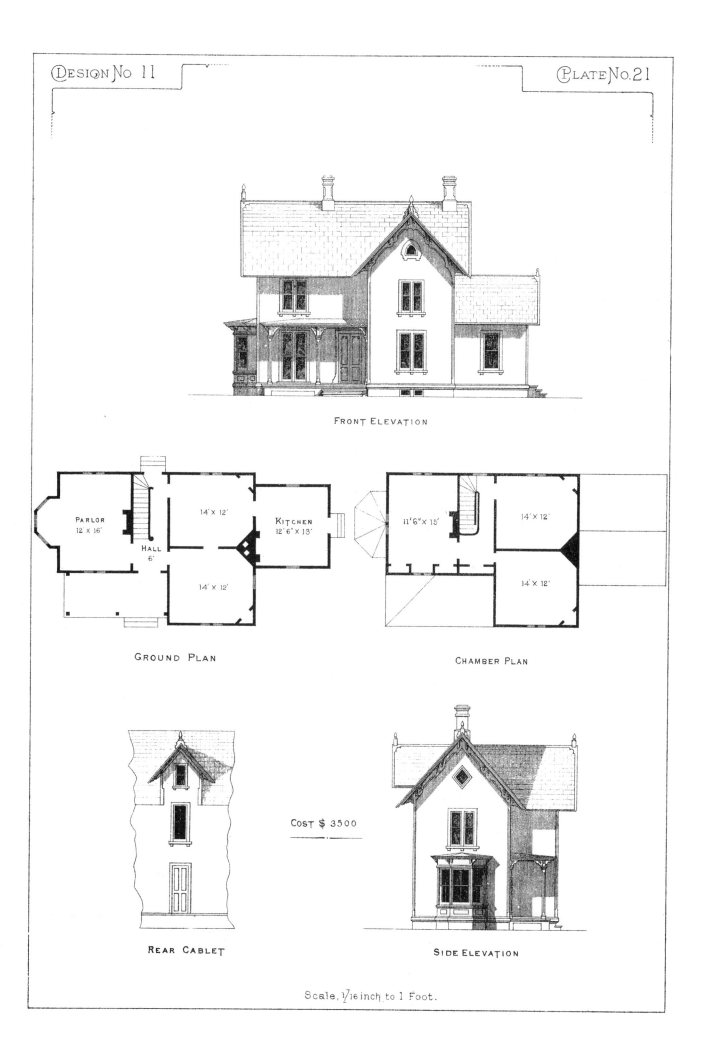

FRONT ELEVATION

GROUND PLAN

PARLOR
12' X 16'

HALL
6'

14' X 12'

14' X 12'

KITCHEN
12' 6" X 13'

CHAMBER PLAN

11' 6" X 15'

14' X 12'

14' X 12'

COST $ 3500

REAR CABLET

SIDE ELEVATION

Scale, 1/16 inch to 1 Foot.

PERSPECTIVE

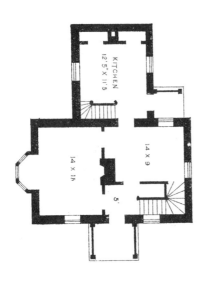

GROUND PLAN

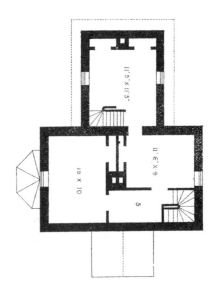

CHAMBER PLAN

Scale ⅛ to 1.

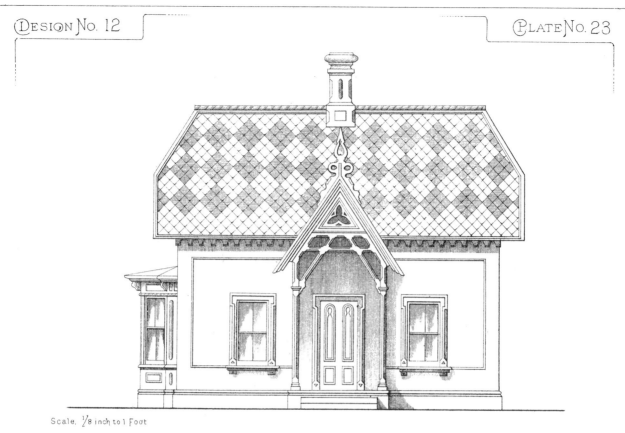

Scale, 1/8 inch to 1 Foot

FRONT ELEVATION

COST IN WOOD $ 3000.

COST IN STONE $ 5000.

SIDE ELEVATION

Scale, 1/16 inch to 1 Foot

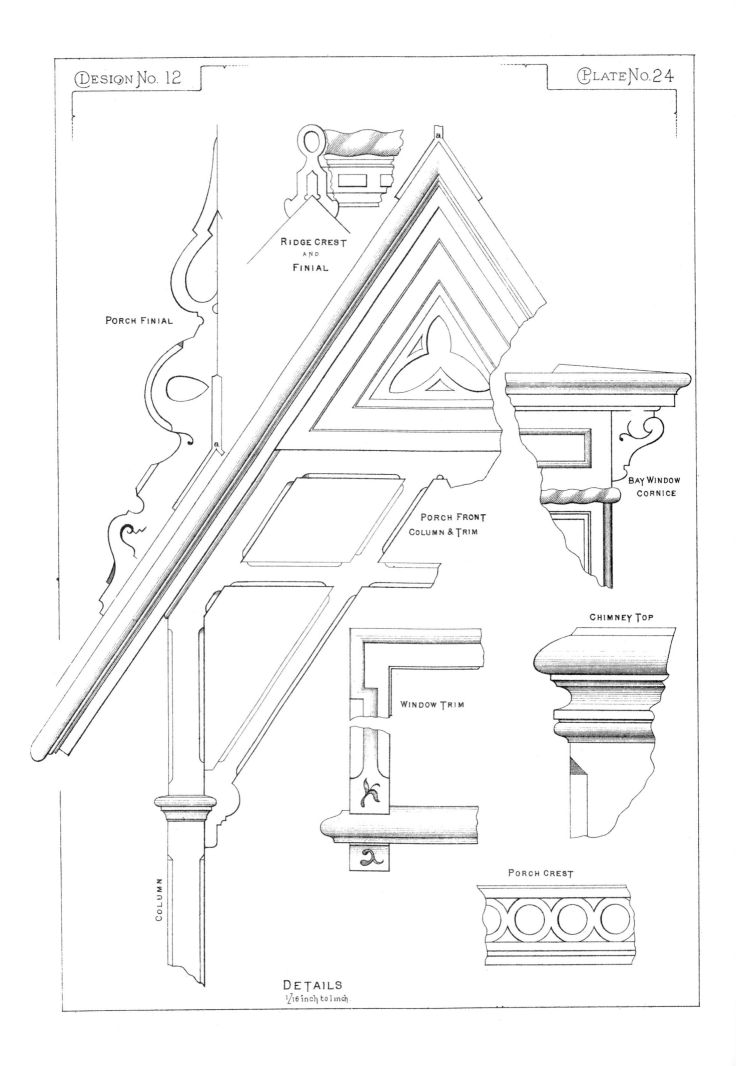

DESIGN No. 12

PLATE No. 24

RIDGE CREST
AND
FINIAL

PORCH FINIAL

PORCH FRONT
COLUMN & TRIM

BAY WINDOW
CORNICE

CHIMNEY TOP

WINDOW TRIM

COLUMN

PORCH CREST

DETAILS
1/16 inch to inch.

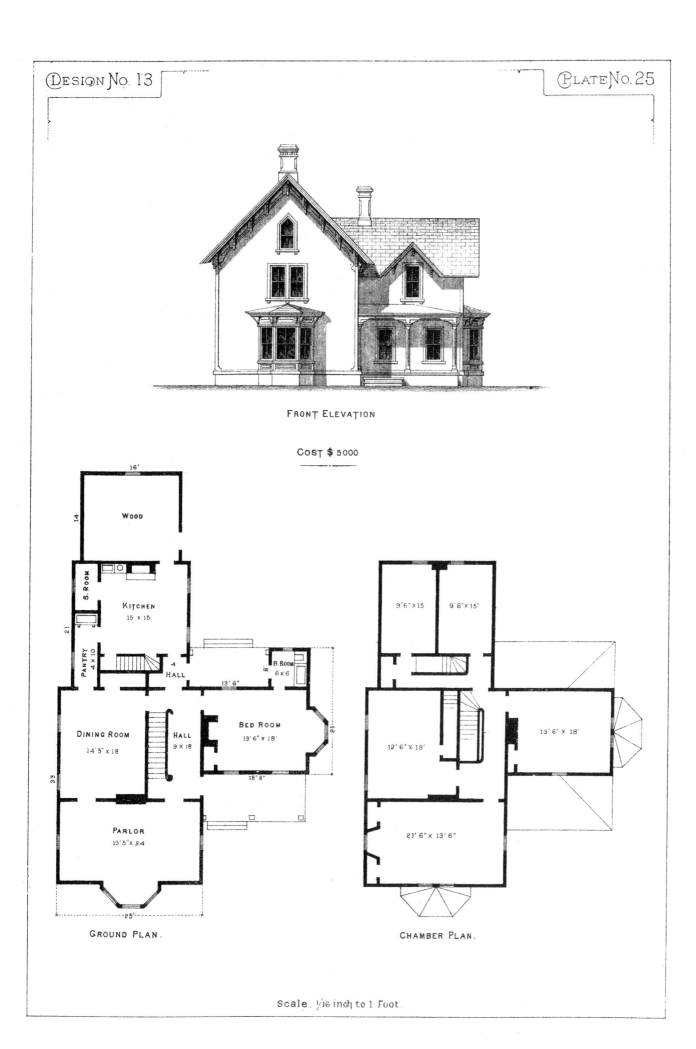

FRONT ELEVATION

COST $ 5000

WOOD

16'

14

S. ROOM

KITCHEN
15 x 15

21

PANTRY
4 x 10

HALL

B. ROOM
6 x 6

13' 6"

8'

DINING ROOM
14' 5" x 18

HALL
9 x 18

BED ROOM
13' 6" x 18'

21

33

18' 6"

PARLOR
13' 5" x 24

25'

GROUND PLAN.

9'6"x15   9' 6"x15'

12' 6" x 18'   13' 6" x 18'

21' 6" x 13' 6"

CHAMBER PLAN.

Scale, 1/16 inch to 1 Foot.

SIDE ELEVATION.

SIDE ELEVATION.

SCALE, ⅟16 Inch to 1 Foot.

LOWER FRONT.

UPPER FRONT.

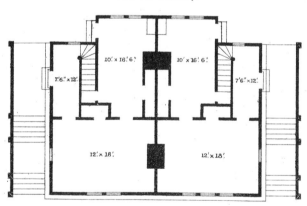

10' x 16' 6"   10' x 16' 6"

7'6" x 12'   7'6" x 12'.

12' x 18'.   12' x 18'.

PRINCIPAL PLAN.

COST IN WOOD & STONE $ 2.000 EACH.

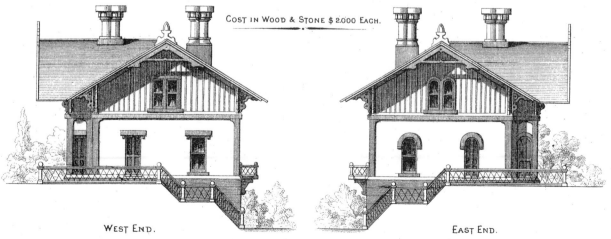

WEST END.

EAST END.

SCALE, 1/16 INCH TO 1 FOOT.

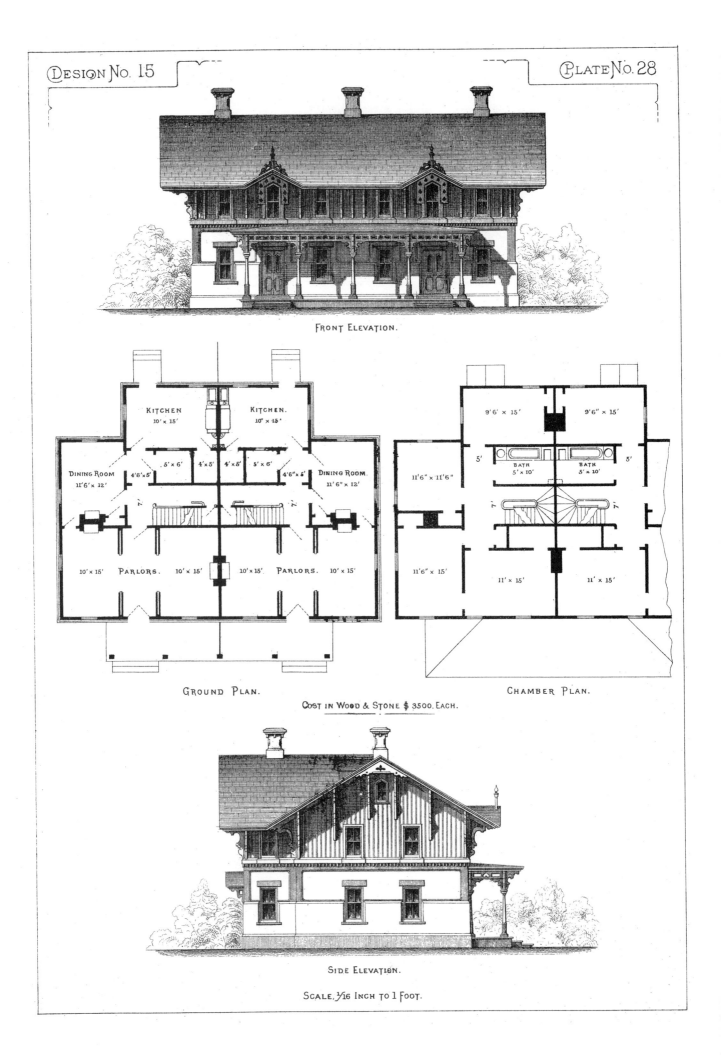

Front Elevation.

KITCHEN
10' x 15'

KITCHEN.
10' x 15'

DINING ROOM
11'6" x 12'

5' x 6'   4'x 5'   4'x 5'   5' x 6'

4'6"x 5'   4'6" x 5'

DINING ROOM
11'6" x 12'

7'   7'

10' x 15'   PARLORS.   10' x 15'   10' x 15'   PARLORS.   10' x 15'

GROUND PLAN.

9'6" x 15'   9'6" x 15'

5'   5'

BATH   BATH
5' x 10'   5' x 10'

11'6" x 11'6"

7'   7'

11'6" x 15'

11' x 15'   11' x 15'

CHAMBER PLAN.

COST IN WOOD & STONE $ 3500. EACH.

SIDE ELEVATION.

SCALE, 1/16 INCH TO 1 FOOT.

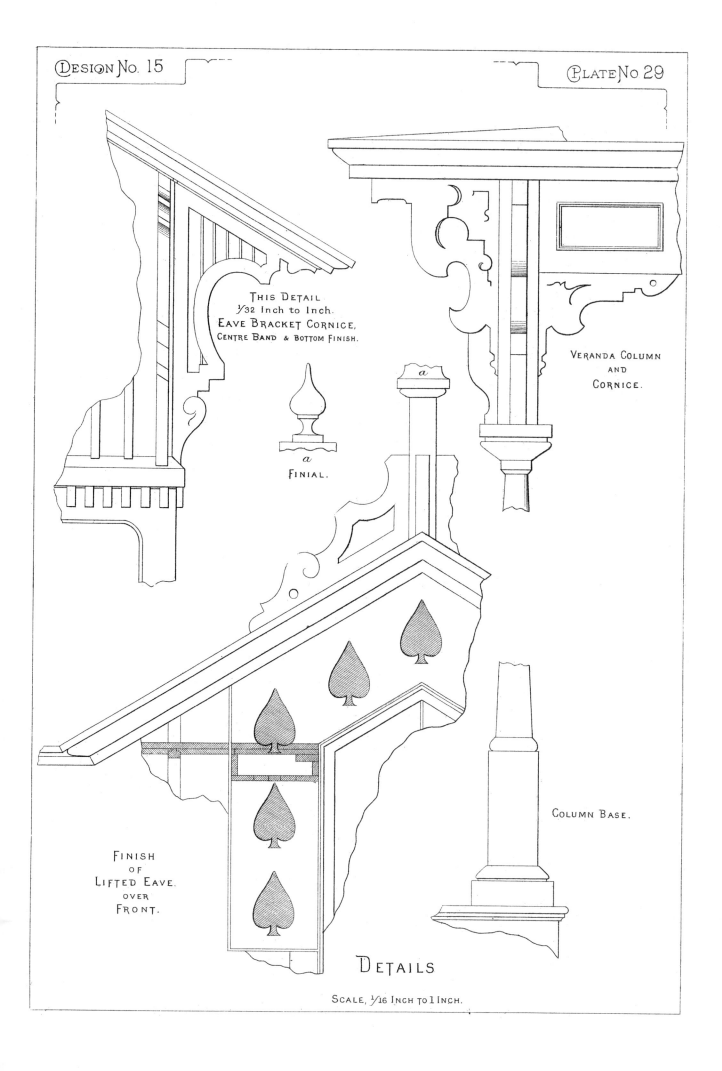

This Detail
1/32 Inch to Inch.
Eave Bracket Cornice,
Centre Band & Bottom Finish.

Veranda Column
and
Cornice.

a
Finial.

Finish
of
Lifted Eave.
over
Front.

Column Base.

Details

Scale, 1/16 Inch to 1 Inch.

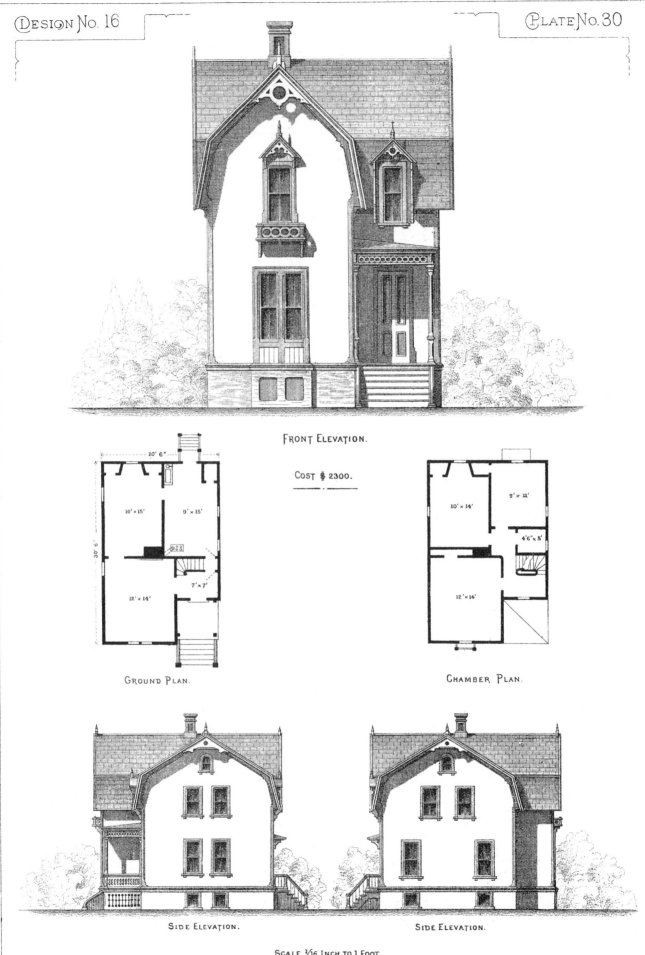

Front Elevation.

Cost $ 2300.

Ground Plan.

20' 6"

30' 6"

10' × 15'   9' × 15'

7' × 7'

12' × 14'

Chamber Plan.

10' × 14'   9' × 11'

4'6" × 5'

12' × 14'

Side Elevation.   Side Elevation.

Scale, ¹⁄₁₆ Inch to 1 Foot.

FRONT ELEVATION

COST $ 2900.

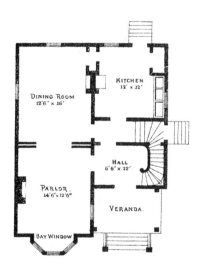

GROUND PLAN.

DINING ROOM
12'6" x 16'

KITCHEN
12' x 12'

HALL
6'6" x 12'

PARLOR.
14'6" x 12'6"

VERANDA.

BAY WINDOW

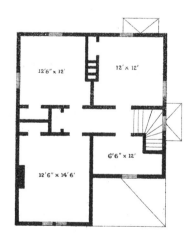

CHAMBER PLAN.

12'6" x 12'

12' x 12'

6'6" x 12'

12'6" x 14'6"

SCALE, 1/16 INCH TO 1 FOOT.

PERSPECTIVE

SIDE ELEVATION.   SIDE ELEVATION.

SCALE, 1/16 INCH TO 1 FOOT.

SIDE ELEVATION.

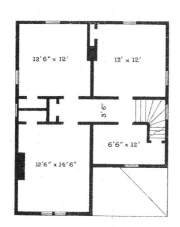

12' 6" × 12'   12' × 12'

3' 6"

6' 6" × 12'

12' 6" × 14' 6"

CHAMBER PLAN.

COST $ 3000.

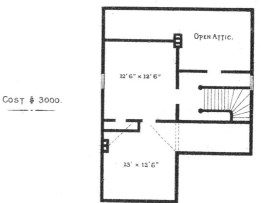

OPEN ATTIC.

12' 6" × 12' 6"

13' × 12' 6"

ATTIC PLAN.

REAR ELEVATION.

SCALE ⅟16" TO 1'.

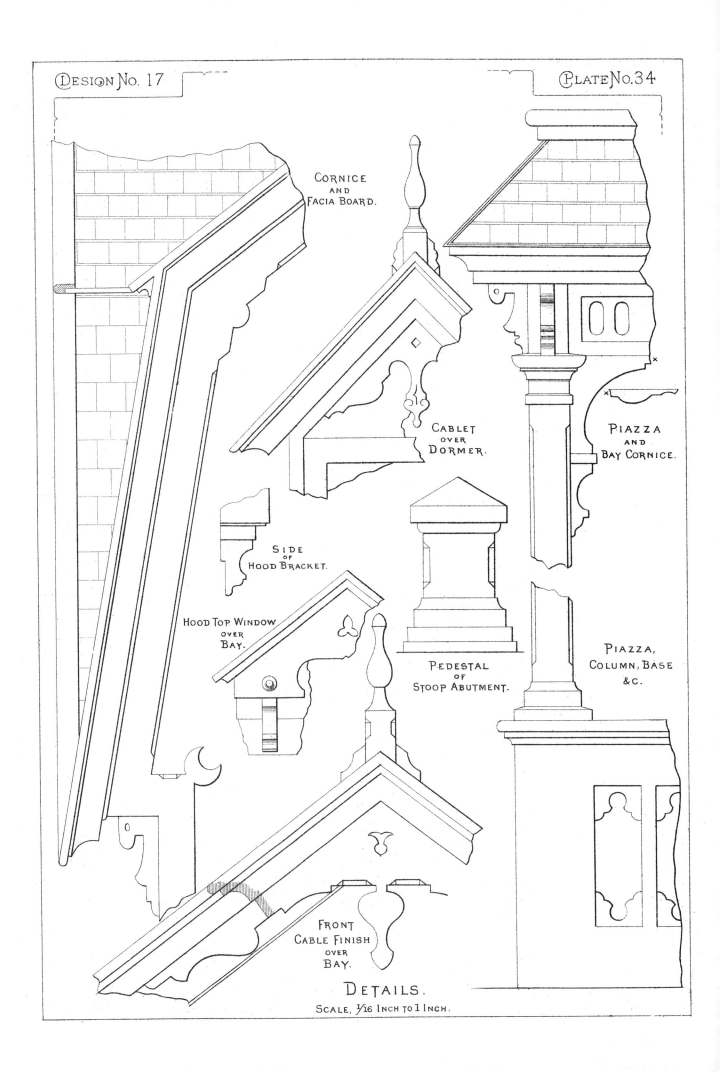

Cornice
and
Facia Board.

Cablet
over
Dormer.

Piazza
and
Bay Cornice.

Side
of
Hood Bracket.

Hood Top Window
over
Bay.

Pedestal
of
Stoop Abutment.

Piazza,
Column, Base
&c.

Front
Cable Finish
over
Bay.

Details.

Scale, ⅟₁₆ Inch to 1 Inch.

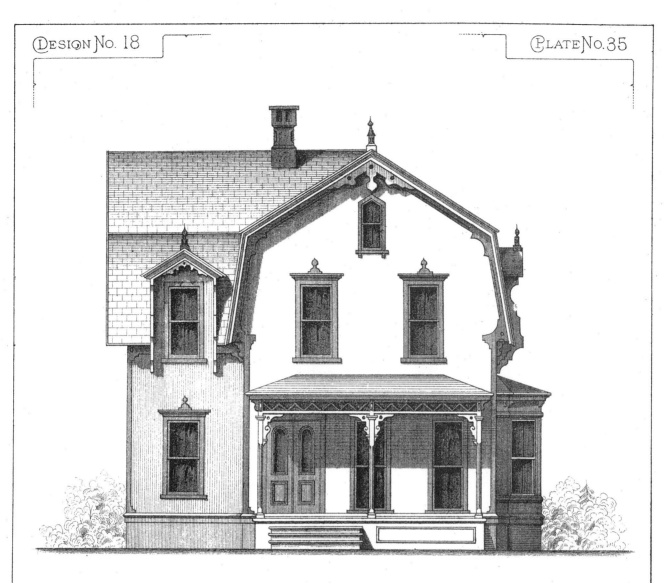

Cost $ 3200

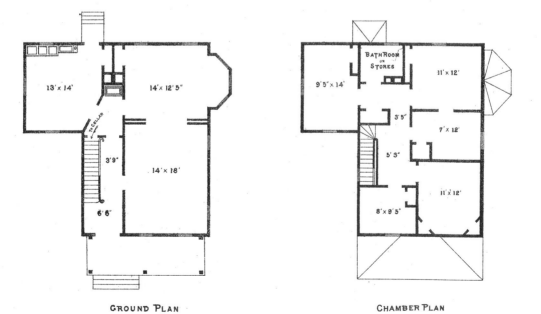

13' x 14'   14' x 12' 5"

TO CELLAR

3' 9"

14' x 18'

6' 6"

Bath Room
or
Stores

9' 5" x 14'   11' x 12'

3' 5"

7' x 12'

5' 3"

8' x 9' 5"   11' x 12'

Ground Plan   Chamber Plan

Scale, 7/16 Inch to 1 Foot

SIDE ELEVATION.

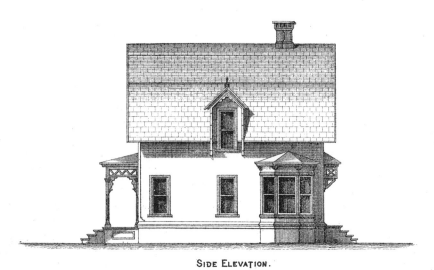

SIDE ELEVATION.

SCALE, 1/8 INCH TO 1 FOOT.   FRONT ELEVATION

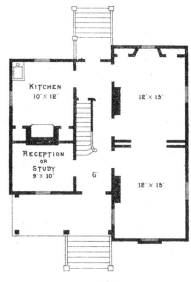

KITCHEN
10' X 12'   12' X 15'

RECEPTION
OR
STUDY
9' X 10'   6'

12' X 15'

GROUND PLAN

4' 10" X 10'   11' 6" X 12'

9' X 10'

5' X 6'   12' X 15'

CHAMBER PLAN

COST $ 4200

SCALE, 1/16 INCH TO 1 FOOT.

PERSPECTIVE

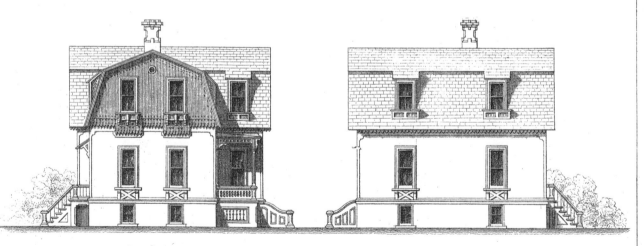

SIDE ELEVATION.   SIDE ELEVATION.

Scale, 1/16 Inch to 1 Foot.

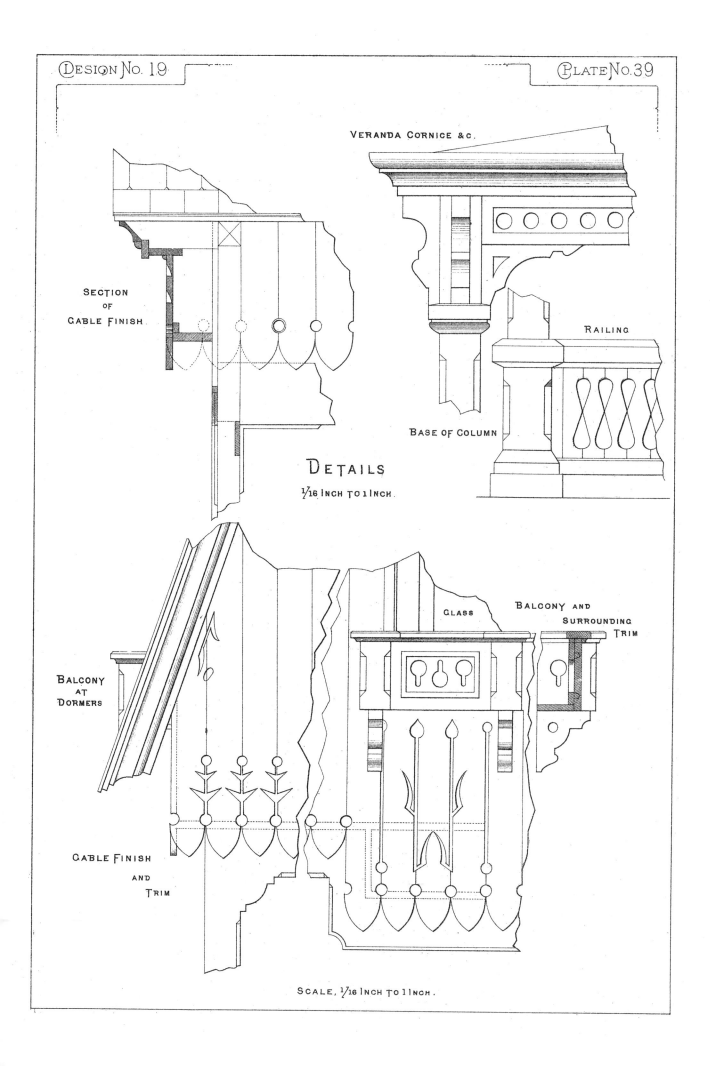

VERANDA CORNICE &c.

SECTION
OF
GABLE FINISH.

RAILING

BASE OF COLUMN

DETAILS

1/16 INCH TO 1 INCH.

GLASS

BALCONY AND
SURROUNDING
TRIM

BALCONY
AT
DORMERS

GABLE FINISH
AND
TRIM

SCALE, 1/16 INCH TO 1 INCH.

FRONT ELEVATION

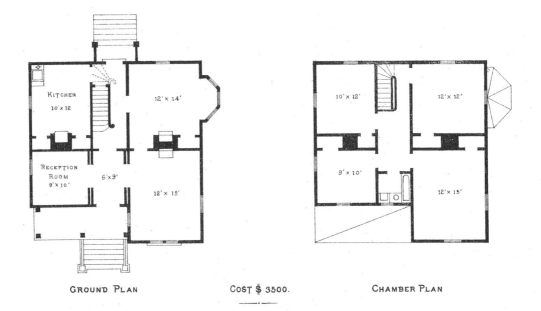

KITCHEN
10' x 12

12' x 14'

RECEPTION
ROOM
9' x 10'

6' x 9'

12' x 15'

10' x 12'

12' x 12'

9' x 10'

12' x 15'

GROUND PLAN

COST $ 3500.

CHAMBER PLAN

SCALE, 1/16" TO 1 FOOT

PERSPECTIVE

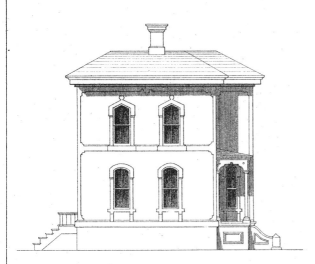

SIDE ELEVATION

SIDE ELEVATION

SCALE, 1/16 TO 1 FOOT

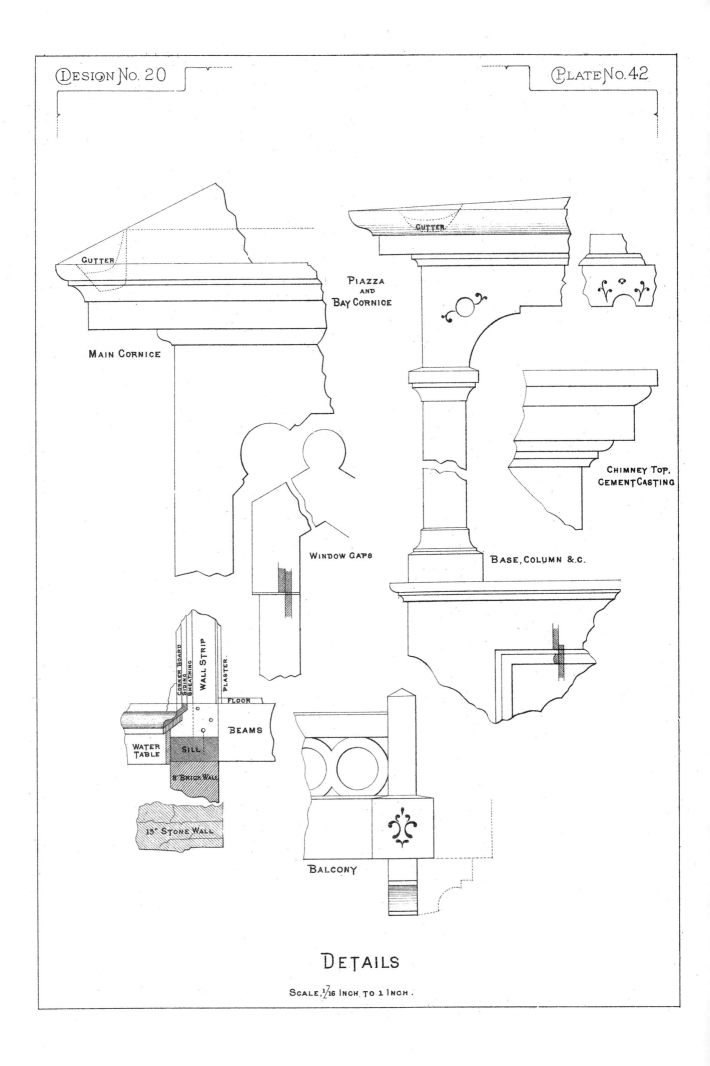

Gutter

Main Cornice

Piazza
and
Bay Cornice

Gutter

Chimney Top,
Cement Casting

Window Gaps

Base, Column &c.

Corner Board
Siding
Sheathing
Wall Strip
Plaster
Floor
Beams
Water Table
Sill
8" Brick Wall
15" Stone Wall

Balcony

Details

Scale, $\frac{1}{16}$ Inch to 1 Inch.

PERSPECTIVE

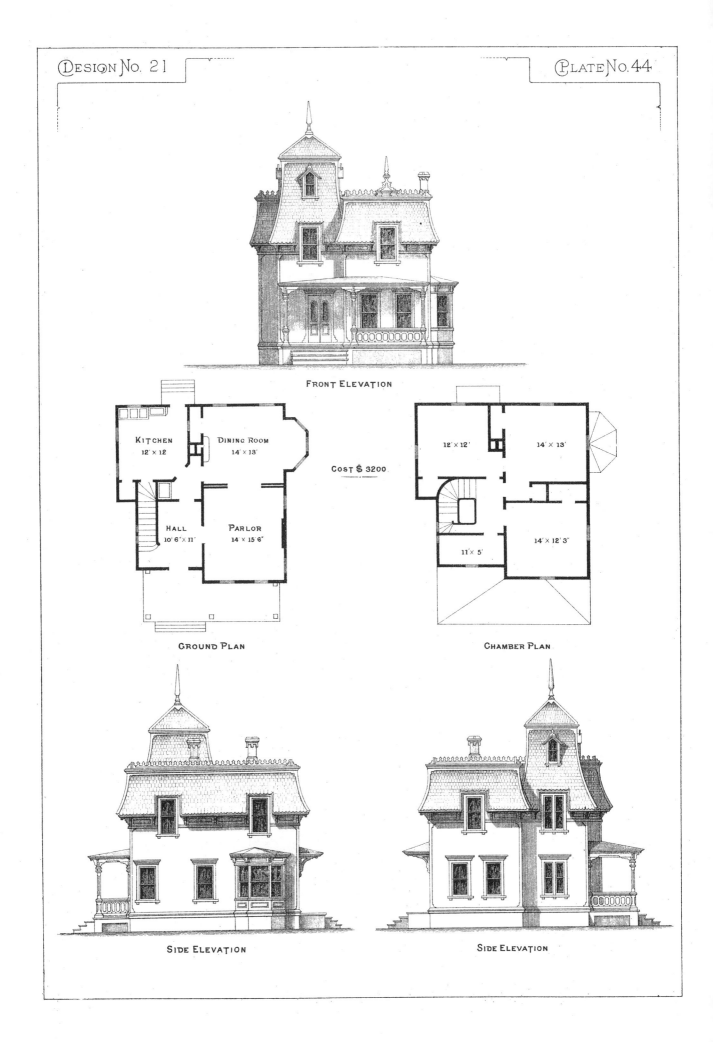

Design No. 21   Plate No. 44

Front Elevation

Kitchen
12' × 12'

Dining Room
14' × 13'

Cost $ 3200

Hall
10' 6" × 11'

Parlor
14' × 15' 6"

Ground Plan

12' × 12'   14' × 13'

11' × 5'   14' × 12' 3"

Chamber Plan

Side Elevation   Side Elevation

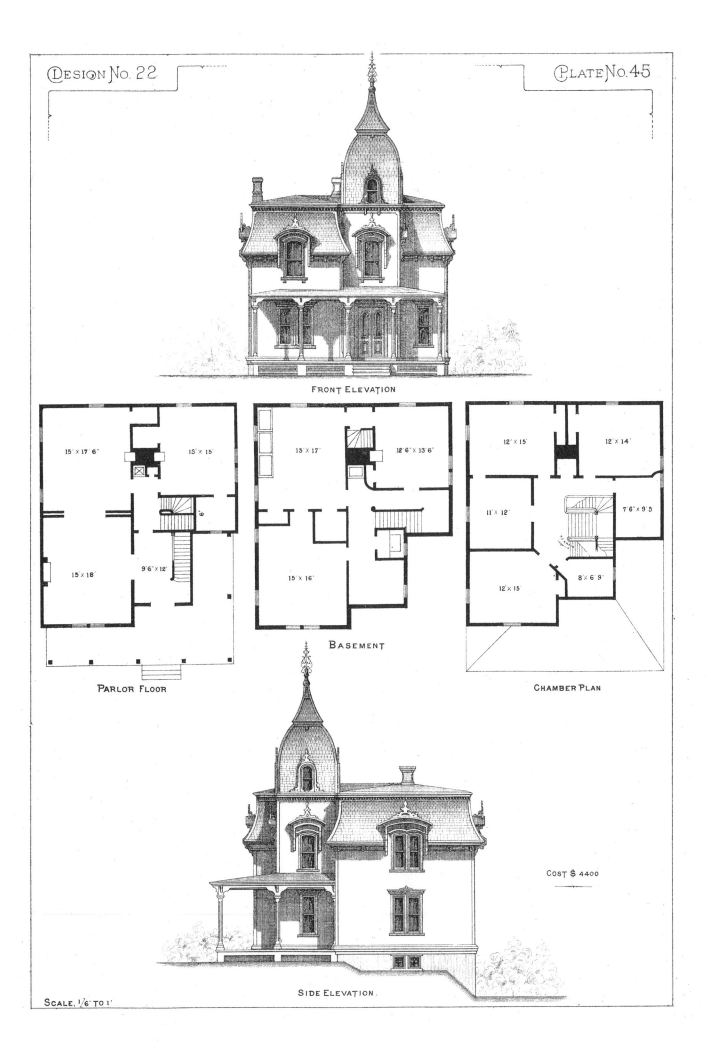

DESIGN No. 22

PLATE No. 45

FRONT ELEVATION

15' X 17' 6"   13' X 15'

6'

15' X 18'   9' 6" X 12'

PARLOR FLOOR

15' X 17'   12' 6" X 13' 6"

15' X 16'

BASEMENT

12' X 15'   12' X 14'

11' X 12'   7' 6" X 9' 5

12' X 15'   8' X 6' 9'

CHAMBER PLAN

COST $ 4400

SIDE ELEVATION.

SCALE, 1/6' TO 1'

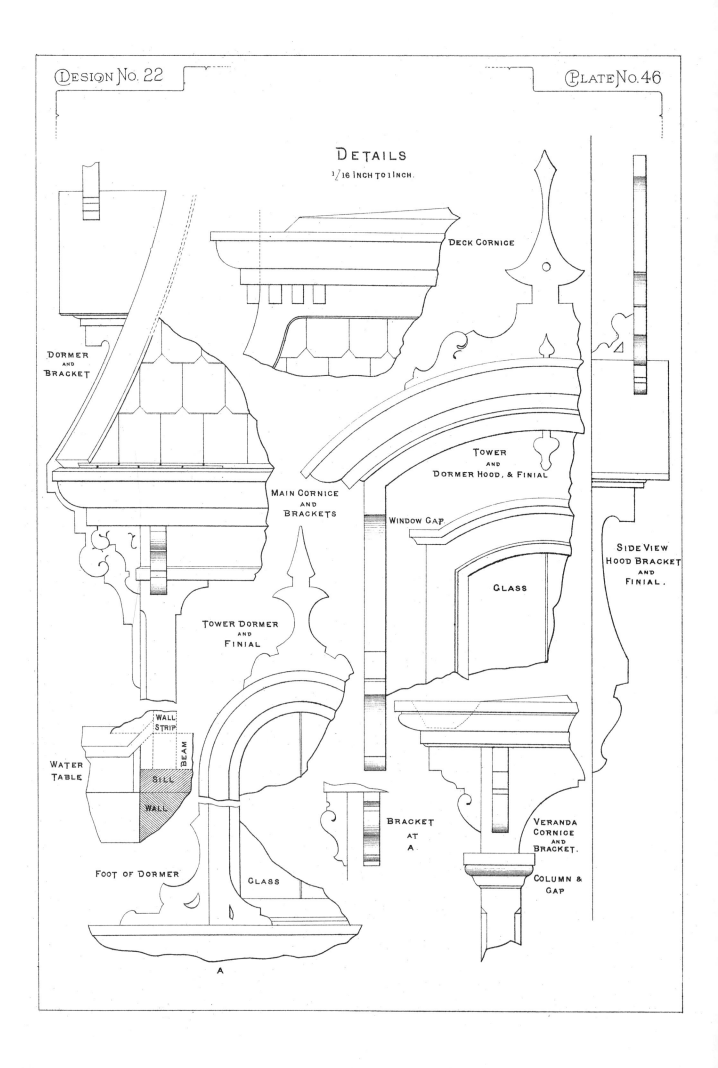

DETAILS

1/16 INCH TO 1 INCH.

DECK CORNICE

DORMER
AND
BRACKET

MAIN CORNICE
AND
BRACKETS

TOWER
AND
DORMER HOOD, & FINIAL

WINDOW GAP

GLASS

SIDE VIEW
HOOD BRACKET
AND
FINIAL.

TOWER DORMER
AND
FINIAL

WALL
STRIP

BEAM

WATER
TABLE

SILL

WALL

FOOT OF DORMER

GLASS

BRACKET
AT
A

VERANDA
CORNICE
AND
BRACKET.

COLUMN &
GAP

A

PERSPECTIVE

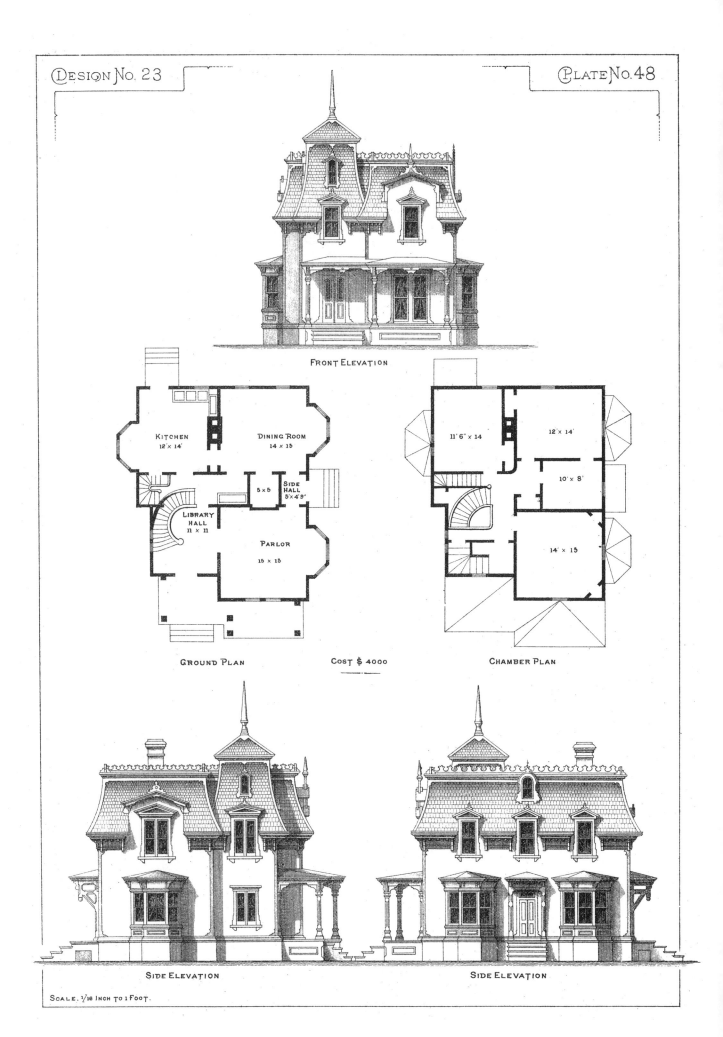

Front Elevation

Kitchen
12' x 14'

Dining Room
14 x 15

5 x 5

Side
Hall
5' x 4'9"

Library
Hall
11 x 11

Parlor
15 x 15

Ground Plan

Cost $ 4000

11' 6" x 14

12' x 14'

10' x 8'

14' x 15

Chamber Plan

Side Elevation

Side Elevation

Scale, 1/16 Inch to 1 Foot.

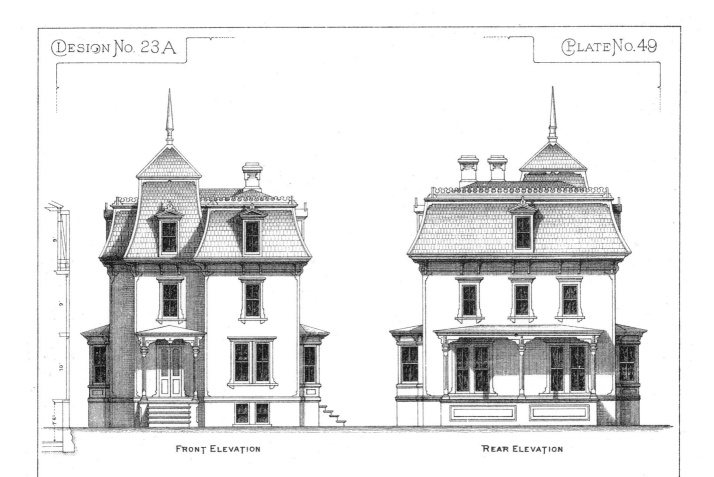

FRONT ELEVATION   REAR ELEVATION

Cost $ 5000

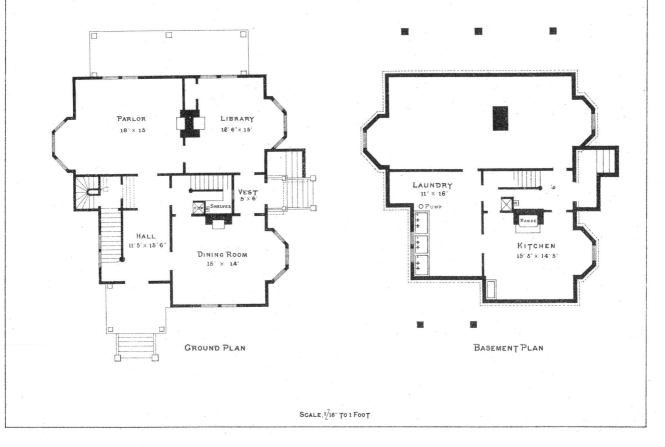

PARLOR
18' x 15

LIBRARY
12' 6" x 15'

VEST
5' x 6'

SHELVES

HALL
11' 5" x 13' 6"

DINING ROOM
15' x 14'

GROUND PLAN

LAUNDRY
11' x 16'

O PUMP

RANGE

KITCHEN
15' 5" x 14' 5"

BASEMENT PLAN

SCALE, 1/16" TO 1 FOOT

SIDE ELEVATION   SIDE ELEVATION

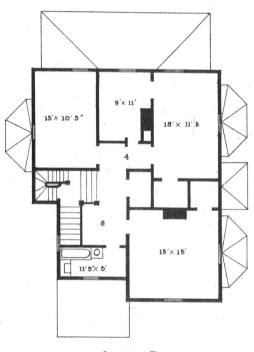

CHAMBER PLAN

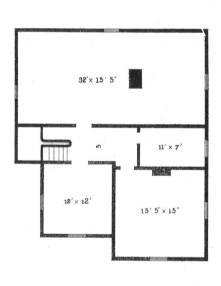

ATTIC PLAN

SCALE, 1/16" TO 1 FOOT.

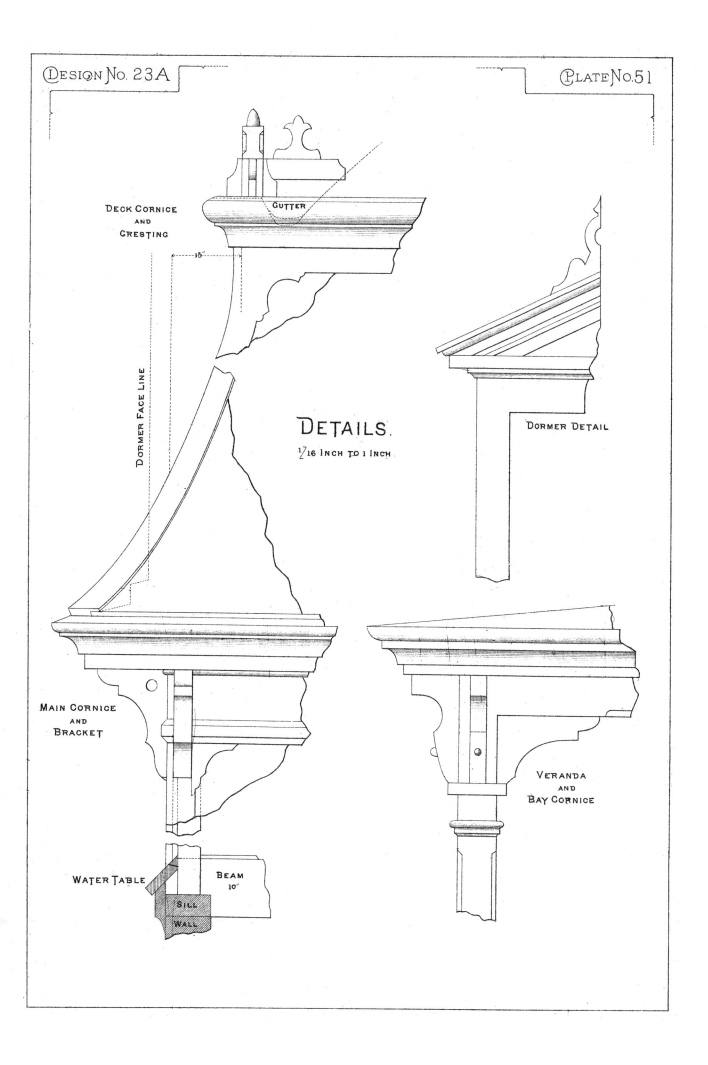

DECK CORNICE
AND
CRESTING

GUTTER

DORMER FACE LINE

15"

DETAILS.
1/16 INCH TO 1 INCH.

DORMER DETAIL

MAIN CORNICE
AND
BRACKET

VERANDA
AND
BAY CORNICE

WATER TABLE

BEAM
10"

SILL

WALL

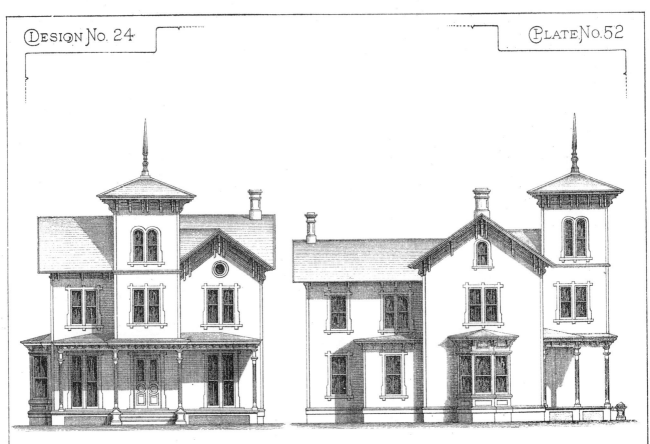

FRONT ELEVATION   SIDE ELEVATION

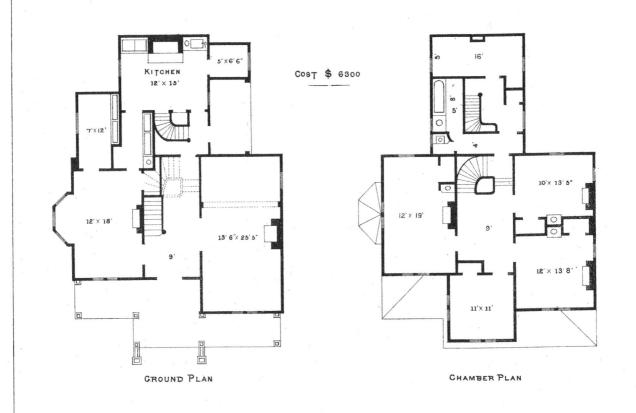

KITCHEN
12' X 15'

5' X 6' 6"

COST $ 6300

7' X 12'

12' X 18'

13' 6" X 25' 5"

9'

5'   16'

8'

5'

10' X 13' 5"

12' X 19'

9'

12' X 13' 8"

11' X 11'

GROUND PLAN   CHAMBER PLAN

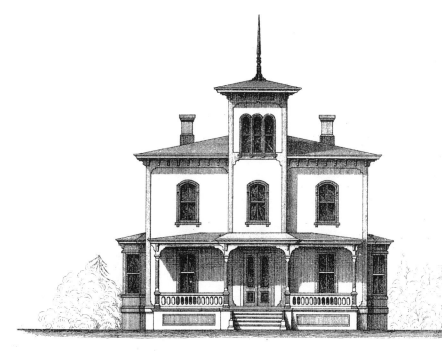

FRONT ELEVATION

COST $ 6000

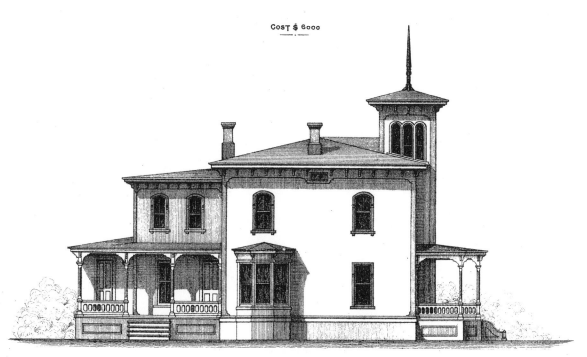

SIDE ELEVATION

SCALE, 1/16 INCH TO 1 FOOT.

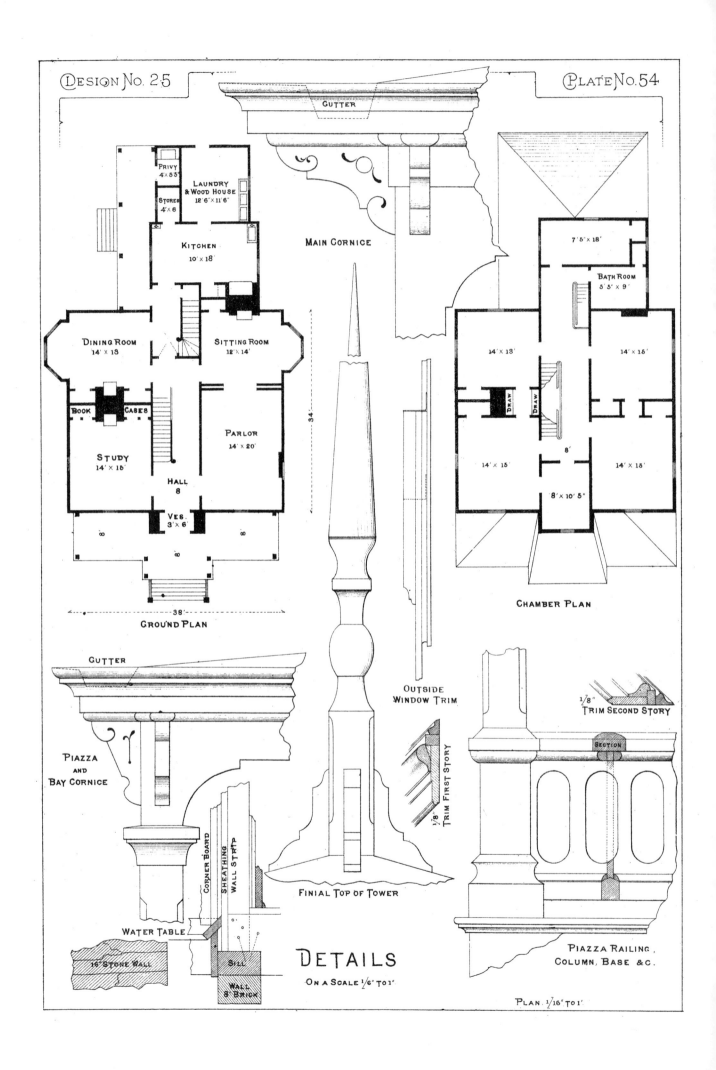

Design No. 25   Plate No. 54

Gutter

Main Cornice

PRIVY
4' x 5.5'

LAUNDRY
& WOOD HOUSE
12'6" x 11'6"

STORES
4' x 6'

KITCHEN
10' x 18'

DINING ROOM
14' x 18'

SITTING ROOM
12' x 14'

BOOK   CASES

STUDY
14' x 15'

PARLOR
14' x 20'

HALL
8

VES.
3' x 6'

34'

38'

GROUND PLAN

7' 5" x 18'

BATH ROOM
5' 5" x 9'

14' x 13'

14' x 15'

DRAW

DRAW

14' x 15'

14' x 15'

8'

8' x 10' 5"

CHAMBER PLAN

Gutter

PIAZZA
AND
BAY CORNICE

CORNER BOARD

SHEATHING

WALL STRIP

WATER TABLE

16" STONE WALL

SILL

WALL
8" BRICK

FINIAL TOP OF TOWER

OUTSIDE
WINDOW TRIM

TRIM FIRST STORY
1/8"

1/8"
TRIM SECOND STORY

SECTION

DETAILS

ON A SCALE 1/6" TO 1'

PIAZZA RAILING,
COLUMN, BASE &C.

PLAN. 1/16" TO 1'

PERSPECTIVE

FRONT ELEVATION

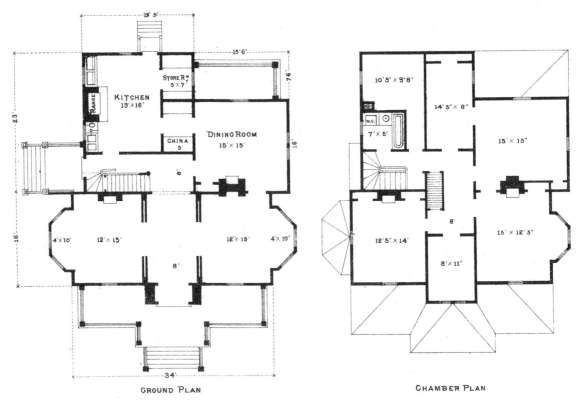

GROUND PLAN

CHAMBER PLAN

COST $ 7000.

SCALE, 1/16 INCH TO 1 FOOT.

SIDE ELEVATION

SIDE ELEVATION

SCALE. 1/16 INCH TO 1 FOOT.

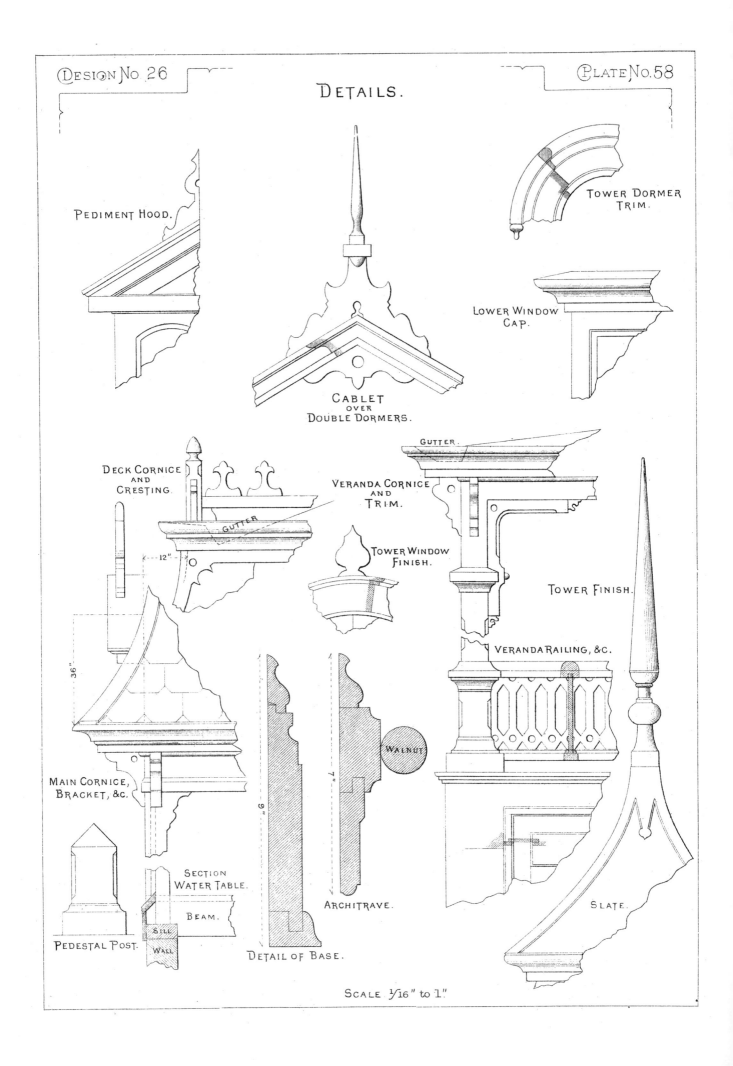

DETAILS.

PEDIMENT HOOD.

TOWER DORMER TRIM.

LOWER WINDOW CAP.

CABLET OVER DOUBLE DORMERS.

DECK CORNICE AND CRESTING.

GUTTER.

VERANDA CORNICE AND TRIM.

GUTTER.

TOWER WINDOW FINISH.

12"

TOWER FINISH.

36"

VERANDA RAILING, &C.

MAIN CORNICE, BRACKET, &C.

WALNUT

6"

7"

PEDESTAL POST.

SECTION WATER TABLE.

BEAM.

SILL

WALL

ARCHITRAVE.

DETAIL OF BASE.

SLATE.

SCALE 1/16" to 1".

PERSPECTIVE

FRONT ELEVATION   REAR ELEVATION

COST $ 8000

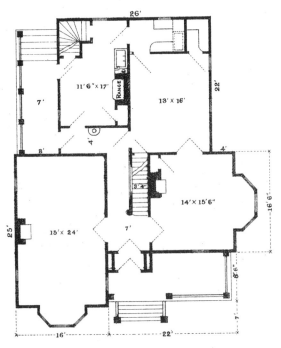

FIRST FLOOR PLAN

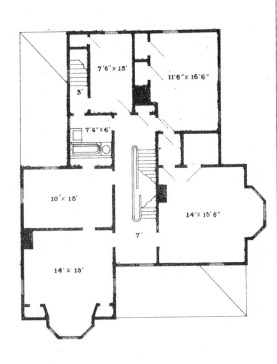

SECOND STORY PLAN

SCALE, 1/16' TO 1'

SIDE ELEVATION

SIDE ELEVATION.

SCALE, 1/16 INCH TO 1 FOOT.

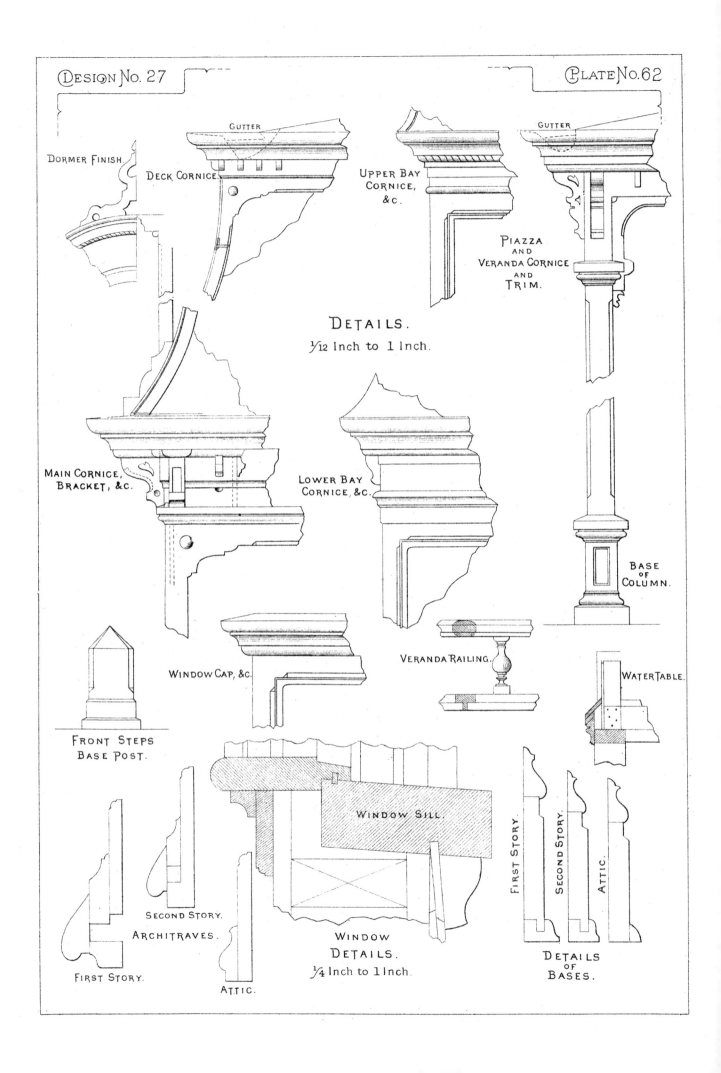

DORMER FINISH.

GUTTER

DECK CORNICE.

UPPER BAY CORNICE, &c.

GUTTER

PIAZZA
AND
VERANDA CORNICE
AND
TRIM.

DETAILS.
1/12 Inch to 1 Inch.

MAIN CORNICE,
BRACKET, &c.

LOWER BAY
CORNICE, &c.

BASE
OF
COLUMN.

WINDOW CAP, &c.

VERANDA RAILING.

WATER TABLE.

FRONT STEPS
BASE POST.

WINDOW SILL.

FIRST STORY.

SECOND STORY.

ATTIC.

SECOND STORY.

ARCHITRAVES.

FIRST STORY.

ATTIC.

WINDOW
DETAILS.
1/4 Inch to 1 Inch.

DETAILS
OF
BASES.

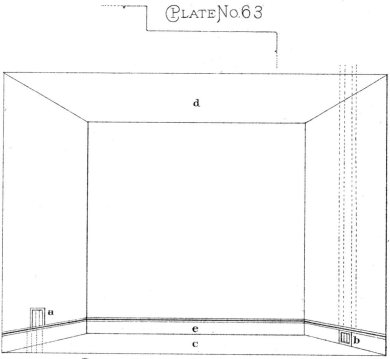

PLATE No. 63

DIAGRAM, SHOWING PROPER METHOD OF HEATING, AND

VENTILATING ROOMS

a. Hot air register   c. Floor.
b. Ventilating flue & register d. Ceiling.

e. Base board .

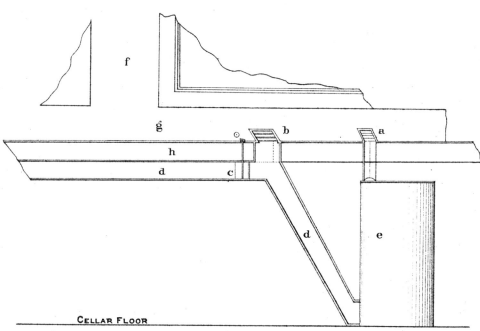

CELLAR FLOOR

DIAGRAM, SHOWING PROPER METHOD OF ARRANGING FURNACE WITH HOT

AND

COLD AIR PIPES & c.

a. Hot air register.   e. Furnace.
b. Cold air register.   f. Room door.
c. Cold air damper, worked in cross slots in floor at ⊙   g. Hall floor
d. Cold air box.   h. Floor beam.